The Interview Mindset

The Ultimate Guide to Mastering Your Career

MASTER Your CAREER !

Mark James

Written By

Mark James, CPC

Acknowledgments

I want to acknowledge the following expert professionals who have inspired me, and generously provided their input regarding several of the chapters in this book:

Marshall Goldsmith, Author, The Earned Life – Leadership

Mark Faust, Author; High Growth Levers – Executive Coaching

Jim Trunick, Author; The Core of Leadership – EQ

Amy Rasdal, Author; Land a Consulting Project NOW! – Plan B

Fred Dawn, Executive Career Coach – The CEO Interview

Ted Robison, aka "Mr. Link Me In" – LinkedIn Coach

Dedication

This book is dedicated to my loving parents, Daniel and Corinne James. Without their encouragement, belief, faith, love, and prayers, I would never have experienced the blessings of exploring the many chapters in my life and career. You both taught me to live the dream; *Love what I do - so I never have to work another day in my life.* **You are the best!**

Endorsements

"This book is an absolute must-read if you are looking for a new job or improving your career path management! Mark James is one of the nation's foremost authorities on what it takes to get a job in today's market."
~Dr. Marshall Goldsmith, Executive Coach and New York Times bestselling author of Triggers, Mojo, and What Got You Here Won't Get You There.

"Some books will address how to answer questions in interviews, others address social media tools, but there is not a book out there that will show you as many tools to use in as short of a read. This is a toolbox for those in top management who are ready to advance in their career through their next move. Mindsets come from confidence in your tools. These tools give you the Interview Mindset."
~Mark Faust, CEO of Echelon Management and the author of High Growth Levers - How the Turnaround Mindset Propels Your Company

"The Interview Mindset shows us how to deliver a real sense of professional honesty, ethics, and integrity required in today's business. I truly respect Mark James' perspective. His career and job search expertise has set the standard with clear and effective career advice."
~Jim Trunick, AIIR Executive Coach and Author, The Core of Leadership

"If you are looking for a new job or improving your career path management The Interview Mindset is a must-read. It's a thoroughly enjoyable and useful book to find your true north once again! I truly respect Mark James' work. Both of his books have helped hundreds of executives chart their career path with increased confidence."

~Amy Rasdal, Founder, Billable at the Beach® and author of Land a Consulting Project NOW!

"Read this book to stay ahead of the pack with more confidence, knowledge transfer, and inspiration to master the art of conducting a successful job interview. If you are serious about your career, read this book and stand out from the crowd during your interviews, land the job, and get paid what you are worth. *The Interview Mindset* gives excellent interview tips and insights. Read and follow this book; it will help make you a better candidate and eliminate the competition for the job you deserve."

~Fred Dawn, Senior Vice President, Lee Hecht Harrison – Retired

"Mark James is brilliant in his depth and breadth of career management expertise. He stands above the rest when it comes to his knowledge of how to improve your job interviews. *The Interview Mindset* provides insightful tips to take control and master your career."

~Ted Robison, aka *"Mr. Link Me In"* LinkedIn and Job Search Coach

Table of Contents

Introduction

Mike has been a full-time Director of Supply Chain Operations for ten years and is interviewing for a newly created VP Operations position at a highly reputable company. During the job interview, his potential boss (the COO) asks: "How can you make an immediate impact here?"

Mike had a good answer for a similar question but was slightly thrown off by how the question was framed. He panics and freezes for a few seconds but then goes back to his mindset and remembers that the position he's interviewing for was created to make the COO job easier.

Mike tells the interviewer, "I see myself immediately fitting into one of your critical initiatives: Raising the inventory accuracy. I was in charge of leading that very same effort at my previous employers, and the plan I created led to outstanding results. I can be ready to take this off your plate starting on day one."

He continues, with even more confidence in his voice: "One part of the job that I'm especially excited about is working closely with the logistics team. I'd be the person you could turn to get a pulse on what's going on in each department. I have a unique perspective on companies' supply chain challenges during these difficult times. I want to use my experience and knowledge to help everyone be more efficient and have their voices heard." He adds that, on his first day, he would schedule meetings with every department leader and listen to their concerns and what kind of support they needed.

What makes Mike's response so great? First, it focuses on how he would make the COO's job easier — by taking leadership in improving current conditions and serving as a liaison for all departments. Second, he reiterated his professional background, priorities, and leadership style.

The Power of The Interview Mindset in a Job Interview

This book will review all of the tools and advice I have collected over the years, providing career transition coaching for hundreds of executives and professionals. Although we're living through testing times, there is a reason to be optimistic – after all; you're most likely reading this book because you have an interview lined up. So well done!

It's now up to you to decide which approach will have the best consequences for you. Will you prepare for the interview thinking: "I'm so nervous," "I hope they like me," or "What if they ask impossible questions?" Or will you instead affirm that you are capable and prepared for success? Navigating your next interview with a positive and constructive mindset is essential.

The Power of The Interview Mindset could make all the difference during your interview. You'll feel confident that you deserve to be there, with the knowledge that you stand just as much chance as anyone else of being offered the job.

Interview the Interviewer

Interviews are also a chance for you to evaluate a potential employer. You are deciding whether you want to work for them just as much as they are deciding whether they want you to work for them. Try putting yourself in this mindset and see if it changes your focus. The Interview Mindset will allow you to enjoy your interview more and portray your authentic self from start to finish – a person who is confident, articulate, and fully deserving of this excellent opportunity. Ultimately, that's who you are, so don't doubt that you are anything else.

Chapter 1

Get LinkedIn or Get Left Out

It's been said that LinkedIn is the 800-pound gorilla. As of today, LinkedIn is the world's largest professional network with 810 million members in more than 200 countries worldwide. My first exposure to LinkedIn began in 2003 when I was invited by a colleague to join. Back then, I was very skeptical. I didn't think it would last, that it was just another social media fad. Boy, was I wrong! But I became one of the first 1.3 million subscribers.

In the beginning, I didn't really embrace it. I wanted them to prove to me whether or not this thing was really going to take flight. But after a while, I started to realize that people want, or even need, to connect. Within a year, I got my first 500 connections. I just languished around that for quite a while until I decided to start my own business. That's when I realized that there's a whole new way to communicate with people out there that you would never be able to reach. And LinkedIn is the perfect tool for career management, as well as managing your own consulting business. It's the perfect arrow in the quiver for what I do, as well as for millions of people who are either planning to make a job change or trying to increase their visibility with regard to being sought out by recruiters. Over the years, it's been proven that LinkedIn is the number one tool for recruiters. They use it almost exclusively as their database to locate, assess and find candidates for jobs.

When I first started, I didn't make myself familiar with the steps to truly make LinkedIn work for me. I underestimated its worth. Several years later, a self-taught LinkedIn expert and now longtime friend, Ted

Robison, aka Mr. Link Me In, showed me a bunch of tips and tricks to maximize my profile. He taught me about keywords, using the banner headline properly, how to beef up my summary, how to add more substance, and how to gain more followers. My LinkedIn profile ranking went from page 26 to page 1 based on my keywords. More on that later. Now I consider myself a power user. I'm on it for at least an hour every day. First thing in the morning, I check the feed, which comes through based on the items that are getting attention. Here you can make comments or you can post your own or hit the like button as many times as you want. Your participation is what gets you ranked higher. Your daily activity on LinkedIn will generate more views of your profile, and potential connections to the people that view your profile.

Now I am able to help my clients through LinkedIn. The first thing I do with any new client is to lay out the structure of how we are going to work together, which is processed in four separate phases. The first phase is administrative; it's preparing the strategy and the plan for the job search campaign. The first thing we're going to do is optimize the resume, getting it perfected for a professional job search campaign, and making sure that bullets are created as an action equaling a result - accomplishment statement. Once the resume is completed, we mirror the resume with their LinkedIn profile. This whole process is all about visibility and credibility. If you look good on paper and you look good on social media (LinkedIn), it's a good bet that you're going to be a credible candidate for a potential job, whether you're found by a company, or by an HR professional, or an executive search recruiter.

There used to be a little stigma with bragging too much about your previous experiences. Now, it's quite the opposite; the more you can project expertise, the more valuable it is throughout your career. Post interesting articles that are relevant to your job search. Once you optimize your profile correctly, then you will get noticed and be found.

As a recruiter, I have placed a number of unemployed people who had been out of work for good reasons. They just happened to be the best-qualified candidate who got the job offer out of the pool of other people who had jobs. It all boils down to who's qualified and who looks great on paper. It will get you noticed and hopefully lead to an interview. And what the final stages of the hiring process ultimately come down to is, *how well do they like you? How well do you fit in or match with the existing team?* So, it's all about the likability factor, which I talked about in my first book.

LinkedIn is also using videos now pretty regularly, and I encourage my clients to use them on their profiles. It will give you extra visibility awareness and ranking when you upload on LinkedIn. It's a great way to add more substance to your profile. Besides showing your expertise, it also shows that you're technologically savvy.

The key is to ramp up your visibility and make sure that people are getting input from you. If they put something out there on their own, like it, comment on it, or put something out that you have created. If you see something on Forbes, Inc, Harvard Business Review, Wall Street Journal, or something that's significant to you, don't just share it. Throw an observation into the comment so people can see why you're posting it. Have your own thoughts in the comments before people click on the link to read it.

The first thing I do when I'm thinking about working with a new person or a new company is to go to their LinkedIn. And then after that, I google them. When I have a meeting, or I'm going to meet a new prospect, or I just met someone at an event, I want to see how they present themselves on LinkedIn. And you can get a multitude of different types of information from LinkedIn if they've completed their profile, or you'll get nothing from them if they haven't done a good job at optimizing their profile. A few years ago, over 50% of the job candidates were getting contacted because of their social media profiles. I know for a fact that I don't even want to ask for a resume as a recruiter until I've looked at someone's LinkedIn profile online. Did I mention that almost 100% of all recruiting firms are using LinkedIn as their primary database?

It is essential not to give too much publicity to your old company in your banner headline, which I see is a big mistake. It says, "People look at me, I work for IBM," or "Look at me. I'm a VP." They think that they're being clever, but they're really missing opportunities by not inserting their category of expertise, or what's in it for the company, or what kind of service they provide. Your banner is the most valuable real estate. What do you do better than anyone on this side of the equator? If it's not clearly explained in your LinkedIn headline banner, people are just going to pass you by. You would think that when someone is looking through profiles, they're looking to find the right person. But it's been my experience that what they're looking for is a reason to disqualify you.

To reiterate, across the world, today's biggest organizational challenge is talent. Finding it. Retaining it. Optimizing it. There's a major exodus of employees changing jobs or leaving the workplace altogether. Organizations need help retaining the talent they have, finding new talent to fill open roles, and ensuring they have the leadership they need to move forward. Many are turning to interim executives as a solution. And for interim executives seeking new roles, the conditions have never been better.

What's required: Clear differentiation and confident self-promotion.

To stand out in an increasingly competitive environment, you need to become an expert at promoting yourself. And it goes farther than simply having a great resume and CV (although that's important, too). You also need to know how to stand out on the world's largest professional online networking platform—LinkedIn.

What To Say on LinkedIn When You've Been Laid Off?

Many people who've been laid off feel like crawling in a hole rather than broadcasting their new job status (or, more accurately, lack of job status) to the world at large. But if you want to find another position, that's precisely what you should do.

In the current economy, with so many talented people being let go, there is "absolutely no shame whatsoever" in clearly indicating that you are out of work. You exude confidence by not being ashamed that you're between jobs. LinkedIn, which functions as an electronic resume, is a valuable tool to help you spread the word.

Until they are laid off, some folks either don't know how to use LinkedIn or have a very skeletal presence on the site. Perhaps they think of it as a job search tool (a mistaken assumption), and either isn't looking or don't want their bosses to think they are. Others are too busy.

Still, while three years ago, senior people thought LinkedIn was for lower-level employees; now, everybody is connected and checking each other out. Often, the first thing people do when they are asked to interview someone – or even just network – is to look the person up on LinkedIn.

If you suddenly find yourself out of work, develop a robust, 100% complete LinkedIn profile. This site is so user-friendly that even newbies ought to be able to find their way. Those who need guidance can rely on LinkedIn's online tutorial or enlist help from an experienced friend or work colleague who has a great optimized LinkedIn profile.

In creating a new profile or editing your current one, be very public about the fact that you're looking for new opportunities. The following are issues to address in these **Key Sections of the LinkedIn Profile:**

Professional Headline

In this line, which goes under your name, give a generic description of what you do or a sample job title (for example, Chief Administrative Officer, Chief Human Resources Officer). Label yourself as what you would like to be, rather than feeling limited by what your last job title was.

Current Position

Since you're now out of work, the "Current" heading should be deleted. Before you do that, though, cut and paste your previous company and job title into the "Past" section. Then click "edit" and "delete," and make the "Current" heading disappear. Don't be concerned that your job shows an end date. It's very acceptable to be in between jobs.

Summary

In a couple of short paragraphs listing your core deliverables, emphasize your key skills and examples of accomplishments. Conclude with a sentence that says, "I am currently looking for new opportunities in a couple of specific functions and industries."

When trying to fill positions that are now open, both headhunters and in-house folks with responsibility for filling a job routinely comb LinkedIn for people who are out of work; it saves them the trouble of having to convince someone who is currently employed to switch jobs. So it's to your benefit to indicate that you're open to new opportunities.

For example, someone who previously worked as a chief administrative officer could write, "Actively pursuing chief administrative officer or chief human resources officer role in a dynamic, collaborative environment." An experienced broker looking to reposition his career into investor relations could say something like, "Currently seeking to leverage my Equity Floor experience and education into Investor Relations." (Alternatively, you can put "Actively seeking new opportunities" in your professional headline.)

Experience

Make sure your descriptions of past jobs adequately convey what you did. Standard rules of resume writing apply here: use active verbs, amply convey your responsibilities, and show results. Since words are scarcer in social media, aim for punchy (think soundbite). Get recommendations from your current or most relevant jobs that reflect varying perspectives — for example, from a manager, a colleague, and a client.

Education

A perennial question is whether people should include graduation dates, which are a tip-off to their age. Executives between their mid-40s and early 60s are discouraged from trying to mask their age.

How do you know when you're finished? When you're in "Edit Profile" mode on LinkedIn, there's a metric that shows the percent of profile completeness. It will make suggestions about what you're missing — whether it's a photo or recommendations. Keep revising until you hit the 100% mark. Then proofread vigilantly.

Once you have found another position, you'll no doubt be eager to update your LinkedIn profile to show where you've landed. But don't neglect it after that. This social media tool is great for sharing updates about what you are doing; your entries on the home page appear at the top of your profile. Think of your LinkedIn page as an active site. You don't want it to go stagnant.

10 Tips to Optimize Your LinkedIn Presence

If it's your goal to land a new job, or secure more consulting clients, or interim/fractional management roles, you have to be very prominent on and active on the #1 social media site in the world.

Here are the **Top Ten Ways to Optimize Your LinkedIn Presence:**

1. Know (and share) your story

What's your greatest talent? Your most valuable deliverable? The thing (or things) you do better than anyone else on this side of the equator? That's your "story" — and it needs to be clearly communicated everywhere you promote yourself, especially on your LinkedIn profile.

2. Define your DNA

That means your **D**rive (what motivates you), your **N**iche (your exclusive area of focus), and your **A**ccomplishments (what sets you apart). Take time to describe how you got to where you're at today and what you can do to satisfy a company's needs and wants.

3. Know your keywords

On LinkedIn, everything revolves around keywords. Whatever it is that defines you (your expertise, deliverables, skill sets, unique value), use those keywords throughout your profile to get a higher ranking during a search. Optimize those keywords by using them repeatedly in different sections.

4. Maximize your banner headline

Your banner headline used to be limited to 20 characters, but it's now been expanded to include more information. The more you can share about your uniqueness and special skills in the headline, the better. Think about sharing a mantra, slogan, philosophy, or whatever you're passionate about.

5. Make (and build) thoughtful connections

When you meet new business colleagues, ask to connect with them on LinkedIn. If you get a connection request, make sure you know them or have a mutual connection. Don't just accept the connection automatically. Take time to introduce yourself and see if there's relevance in the connection. If so, accept the connection, but take it one step further by setting up a phone call or Zoom meeting to get to know each other and see how you may be able to help each other.

6. Harness the power of groups

With the premium LinkedIn membership, you can join up to 50 different groups, including industry associations related to your field (e.g., finance, manufacturing, sales, marketing) or vertical markets you support. Look at discussions, review others' posts and offer your perspective (see formula below).

7. Use the "5-3-1" daily activity formula

One of the best ways to boost your LinkedIn visibility is to take these actions every day (five days a week):

✓ **5 times a day:** "Like" something you see. Look for people who have posted something that you like or agree/align with. Click the like button. It's a great way to get noticed and appreciated.

✓ **3 times a day:** "Comment" on a post you like. Share why you agree, how you can relate to it, or add another idea, suggestion or tip.

✓ **1 time a day:** Post or share one thing new from you. It could be something you wrote or a relevant article you found elsewhere online. Simply post it and add a comment about why it inspires you, why you agree, or any additional perspective that demonstrates your expertise. All of your followers will see the activity, which increases your visibility as a subject matter expert or thought leader.

8. Be diligent and consistent

Commit to doing some activity on LinkedIn five days a week. The activities themselves may be small, but they all add up to much greater visibility over time.

9. Get a professional headshot and a customized background image

Hire a professional photographer to create a "LinkedIn high-resolution headshot" and upload a "unique" banner cover picture behind your headshot at the top of your profile — something related to your industry or vertical market. A Google search will pull up hundreds of free options.

10. Build your bank of recommendations

Offer to recommend your clients, colleagues, or customers, then ask if they would be willing to return the favor. (Most will say yes.)

Biggest LinkedIn Mistakes

It's not only important to know what to do on LinkedIn, but it's also important to know what not to do:

1. No Profile Photo

"An ounce of image is worth a pound of performance - and you only have 50 Milliseconds to make a first impression?"

The absence of a LinkedIn photo can be interpreted as, "I'm too busy to take this seriously." Spend the time and money and get a professional headshot. And look the part; make sure you're dressed with your professional image.

The human brain processes images faster than words. According to HubSpot, the brain processes visual information 60,000 times faster than the time it takes for the brain to decode text. It does this in 1/10 of 1 second. Tie that into the impact you can make with a personal connection. Relationship building online depends on images.

In the internet age, most of the first impressions we make are now online. And that means that photography is more important to businesses than ever before! Visual consistency is the fastest way to tell your present yourself and connect with recruiters, companies, and clients.

A headshot alone is not personal branding but will contribute to your brand. Take the time to get it done professionally. Your social media profile headshot photos should be close-up, recognizable images of you.

Update your LinkedIn banner cover photo. This is the background image at the top of your profile. Recruiters search through hundreds of profiles, and your use of imagery might just get their attention.

Solution: Here are 5 Key Elements of a Good LinkedIn Profile Picture:

- Professionally taken photograph

- Professional attire and dress code
- Cheerful Positive Smile and Attitude
- Current and Recent Photo
- Right size headshot and resolution

2. A boring introductory "Banner Headline"

This title appears right below your photo and name, making it one of the first things people see. Think of this field as your answer to, "What do you do?" BUT, **do not** list your job title!

Your brief reply might be, "Manufacturing and Technology Leadership" OR "I bring next-generation products from design into the marketplace." Be creative and personalize your headline banner with a quote or slogan to stand out.

Solution: Your headline needs to answer three questions:

1) What do you do?
2) Who do you help?
3) How do you help them?

3. Maximize and Optimize your "About" summary

Just like an entrepreneur pitching a startup or a writer trying to introduce a screenplay to a producer, you have an idea to sell. That idea is you.

Use first-person pronounces: It's okay to say "I" — people expect to hear from you directly. Referring to yourself in the third person is for the resume. Your LinkedIn profile should be more personal and strive to make connections. Avoid the over-used buzz phrases and cliches like: "What I bring to the table" OR I'm a team player who enjoys collaborating with others" OR "I am a people person who enjoys working with teams."

Solution: Go one step further by describing what being a "team player" means to you: *"I lead collaborative teams that bring out the best in*

11

others and myself to creatively address problems and brainstorm solutions."

Instead of saying what you bring to the table, try this; *"One of my greatest deliverables is my ability to lead teams, let me give you an example."*

Make it meaningful: While the content of your "About" statement makes it all about you, the connection it makes is all about others. The goal is to present and showcase WHO you are? WHY do you do what you do? HOW are you successful? and WHAT is in it for your next employer?

4. Work Experience section without Substance

Just as with your resume, you should use an accomplishment-first approach. I suggest at least 3-5 action=result bullet accomplishments for every job you have listed on your LinkedIn profile.

Here is a sample of a good bullet structure: "Led a team of twelve colleagues in six countries in launching a new product line that exceeded initial sales projections by 18%."

For your past jobs: Use the same approach, highlighting your top accomplishments. Share credit with your team: If you worked on a project with others, tag their names in your LinkedIn post (especially if you're a mid-level manager who directed the team while others did the work). This in no way dilutes recognition of your efforts.

Incorporate keywords that are relevant to your industry: Employers scan for keywords that indicate your skills and level of expertise. One way to identify these keywords is to read job descriptions in your industry and take note of specific qualifications. Then make sure those same phrases are included in your profile. Keep updating and refreshing your profile as you achieve more accomplishments

5. Not being proactive with "Recommendations"

Endorsements are a great way for building credibility. For example, your profile might show that Bob Smith and five other professionals endorse your social media skills. But recommendations are a huge cut above because they require more than just the click of a button. The most powerful ones are written by genuinely enthused people whose expectations you exceeded. Something to keep in mind: a thoughtful and well-written recommendation from a peer who speaks with specifics can do more to distinguish your profile than generic comments from people who are many levels above you.

Solution: Take the time to personally invite each person to provide you with a recommendation by reminding them of your skills and what you did for them. Read the tutorial on How to ask for a recommendation on LinkedIn.

6. Not enough online Activity
While you want to keep a current and active profile. Keep your LinkedIn activity relevant to your business sector, function, and discipline. The more you post - the higher your LinkedIn ranking. If you are a blogger – upload your posts and comment on other posted articles. But remember – it's not Facebook. No one cares what restaurant you had dinner at last night, or the cute picture of your dog or cat?

Solution: Use the **5-3-1 Formula** daily to become a LinkedIn Power-user:
- Five (5) Likes on other posts
- Three (3) thoughtful comments on other posts
- One (1) New post by you. i.e., shared the article with opening comments, blog posts, etc.

7. Not Editing for Grammar and Typos
The worst thing that can happen is to have a profile that has a lot of poor grammar and typos. Have someone else look at your profile to notice any imperfections.

8. Not Creating a Personalized URL LinkedIn Profile Hyperlink
When you originally subscribed to LinkedIn, your profile link gets added

with extra random (alpha-numeric) letters and numbers that are generated by the computer and added to your URL. You must personalize it with your name. If your name is not available, play with variations. For example, markjames444 or markjames.coaching. My LinkedIn profile is: **https://www.linkedin.com/in/markjamescpc/**

LinkedIn Demographics

Linkedin is a business-oriented social media networking site that enables users to connect with colleagues, look for a new job or business relationship, and get answers to industry questions. Linkedin users are able to invite who they know and trust to become "linked in," and the business connections of invited users are in turn linked.

Still not convinced LinkedIn is right for you? Let's end this chapter with a few statistics:

1. LinkedIn now has almost 810 million members with over 55 million registered companies in over 200 countries worldwide.
2. Of those LinkedIn users who are frequently engaging with the platform, 40% access it on a daily basis, clocking up over 1 billion interactions every month. However, LinkedIn is used sparingly, so you only have a few minutes to make an impact. Users only spend about 17 minutes on LinkedIn per month.
3. According to the Pew Research Center 2018 Social Media Use study, LinkedIn remains popular with college students. Further research into these LinkedIn statistics revealed that 50% of college graduates in the US are LinkedIn users, while the site engages with only 9% of people whose education doesn't surpass high school.
4. Additionally, 44% of LinkedIn users take home more than $75,000 per year, which is above the national median in the US.
5. Although the US has the most LinkedIn users at 176 million, over 75% of LinkedIn users are from outside of the US.

6. Along gender lines, LinkedIn is more popular with men, who comprise 57% of its users base. And interestingly, millennials make up over 60% of LinkedIn's user base, with 11 million of the 87 million millennials in decision-making positions.

7. Microsoft, recognizing the value of LinkedIn, acquired the company for $26.2 billion in 2016. However, unlike many other social media platforms which rely on advertisements, LinkedIn's services are something for which users are willing to pay.

8. A total of 39% of LinkedIn users pay for LinkedIn Premium, which has four price tiers:

   ➢ Premium Career: $29.99/month
   ➢ Premium Business: $59.99/month
   ➢ Sales Navigator Pro: $79.99/month
   ➢ Recruiter Lite (Hiring): $119.95/month

Premium Career is best for those looking for jobs. It gives you access to 10 InMail messages per month and in-demand videos, as well as the ability to see who viewed your profile, how many searches you've appeared in, and additional information on posted jobs. The other tiers include essentially the same basic features but then go a step or two further.

Premium Business gives you additional information about businesses and unlimited people searches. **Sales Navigator Pro** gives you advanced search filters, access to different sales tools, and the ability to make notes on user profiles; and **Recruiter Lite** gives you guided search smart suggestions and more recruiter-focused tools. No matter which premium account you buy, you'll have access to improved metrics and various ways to achieve LinkedIn growth.

9. LinkedIn is an especially good source for discovering leads. Hubspot has found out that LinkedIn is 277% more effective at

generating leads than Facebook and Twitter.

Chapter 2

C SUITE to The Board Seat

All publicly-traded companies and non-profit organizations have a board of directors. Serving on one of these boards is a great way to help improve an organization by using your skillset. Successfully joining a board of directors often requires a dedicated strategy for searching and networking. In this chapter, I will explain what a board of directors does, the benefits of joining one, and the steps you can follow to join your first board.

What is a Board of Directors?

A board of directors is a group of individuals who represent the shareholders of a publicly-traded company or non-profit. It is a governing body that oversees upper management and sets policies for how the organization operates. Legal requirements stipulate that every for-profit and non-profit company has a board of directors. Most company boards range in size from three to 31 members and include both internal members of the organization and external members.

Benefits of Joining a Board of Directors

Joining a board of directors is a common goal for accomplished career professionals who wish to take on another challenge. Sometimes these people are retired and want something challenging to do, while others join a board of directors while they are still working full-time elsewhere. There are several benefits to joining a board of directors, including:

- Additional income
- Networking opportunities

- Professional recognition
- Ability to pursue a cause that's important to you
- Opportunity to improve an organization you believe in
- Need a new career challenge

How to Get on a Board of Directors

To pursue an open position on a board of directors, follow these steps:

1. Build your reputation

People earn positions on boards of directors when they have proven proficiency and expertise in their industry. One option for improving your reputation is to write articles related to your industry. You can also perform speaking engagements on topics you are knowledgeable about. Look for industry-related conferences that are seeking guest speakers or offer to speak at organizations that could use your guidance.

Social media is another way to build your reputation. By sharing useful information and promoting your work in the field, you can attract a larger social following. You can also use professional networking sites to promote your experience and skills.

Building a strong reputation is something that can take time but has long-term benefits. Therefore, it's helpful to start working on your public reputation as early as you can.

2. Develop your network

Anyone looking to eventually join a board of directors should regularly focus on networking opportunities. Doing so provides two unique benefits. First, through your personal and professional network, you might discover open board positions. If someone in your network comes across a board position that is right for you, they inform you of this opportunity.

Second, building your network provides more peer recommendations. Having a very strong relationship with more people in the industry lends credibility to your capabilities.

To develop your network, start by attending networking events as well as conferences in your industry. Keep your connections strong by regularly reaching out to the people you meet. Your network also consists of former and current colleagues, along with your relationships. Let these people know you're looking for a board position and the type of organization you wish to join. When developing connections, remember that it's better to focus on quality over quantity, as close connections are more likely to recommend you for future opportunities.

3. Join organizations

Joining organizations is another good way to get on a board of directors. There are two types of organizations to consider. The first are organizations dedicated to helping people get on boards of directors. There are specific organizations that focus on connecting people with open board positions, helping them apply, and gaining approval to join.

The other type of organization is local non-profits. If there is a cause you care about, joining a non-profit related to this cause is a good way to gain experience serving on a board of directors. It's typically easier to join the board of a smaller non-profit, allowing you to further develop your reputation and your network.

4. Assess each opportunity

As you start to receive opportunities to join boards of directors, assess each opportunity to ensure it suits your time commitment, abilities, and interests. Investigate the opportunity and whether you'll be able to make a significant contribution to the organization. Look at the current status of the organization, its plans, and the other board members for more information. If the opportunity seems like it is a good fit for you, you can accept the invitation to join.

Tips for Joining a Board of Directors

Here are a few tips you can use after joining your first board of directors to make the most of the opportunity:

Study the company

Once joining a board, spend some time learning everything you can about the organization. Study the strategy, the managers involved in the history of the organization, and anything else you can find. It's good to have a thorough understanding of the organization before your first board meeting so you can fully contribute to the conversation.

Start slowly

Joining a board of directors is typically a long-term commitment. Therefore, you can take your time when it comes to making an impact on the organization. Learn the dynamics of the current board members and how they operate. By starting slowly and getting to know your fellow board members, you can form strong collaborations that help you achieve your long-term goals.

Find a unique way to help

Every person brings their unique skills and experiences to a board of directors. After joining, look for what you have to offer that others do not. For example, if you have a strong background in multimedia marketing, you can ask to meet with senior managers in that department and find out how you can help.

Joining a Board of Directors FAQs

Below are some commonly asked questions related to joining a board of directors:

How long does it take to get on a board?

Joining a board of directors is a long-term plan that requires time and strategy. The amount of time it takes to join a board of directors can depend on your experience level, network size, and the type of organization you wish to serve.

Do board members get paid?

At public companies, board members do receive compensation. This can take the form of a base retainer fee along with other benefits such as stock options, stock grants, liability insurance, and reimbursements. Positions on boards at non-profits are more commonly volunteer roles.

What happens if I decide to leave the board?

Positions on boards of directors at public companies are subject to that board's term structure. Commonly, positions run for three-year terms, with a limit of two consecutive terms. If you no longer wish to serve on the board, the typical procedure is to simply wait for your current term to expire.

This is different for volunteer board positions at non-profits. To leave this position, first, inform the board chair and president. After that, let the rest of the board know of your decision. Finally, prepare a formal resignation letter and deliver it to the board president. It's best to give the board as much time as you can so they can make adjustments to your departure.

What skills should I develop to perform well on a board of directors?

A quick list of skills for board members to develop include:

- Leadership
- Board Governance
- Risk Management
- Negotiation
- Conflict Resolution
- Employee Hiring and Retention
- Staff Management
- Diversity and Inclusion
- Finance and Accounting

- Written and verbal communication
- Sales and Marketing

How do Board Members Get Compensated?

The average salary for a board member is **$38,818 per year**, and the average salary of a board of directors is **$67,073 per year**. Board members typically do not receive an hourly salary. Instead, they may get a base retainer fee for their services as a member. In addition to a retainer, some of the compensation options offered to board members include:

- **Stock options:** When offering stock options, the organization gives board members the right to buy and sell a particular number of shares in its stocks at a specific price rather than market value. The board members are not required to utilize their stock options, though the organization sets a predetermined deadline for purchasing and exercising them.
- **Stock grants:** When an organization provides stock grants to board members, it gives them a specific number of shares in its stock at no cost. That ownership may occur at a predetermined timeframe, such as three years. If the board member leaves before the three-year mark, they lose their stock in the organization.
- **Reimbursements:** Board members often receive reimbursement for the costs incurred for traveling to board meetings or retreats. For example, they get compensated for airfare and hotel or other lodging reservations. Some receive a per-diem rate, which provides them a daily allowance for travel-related expenses, including meals.
- **Liability insurance:** Due to the role's responsibilities, an organization may provide liability insurance as part of board members' and directors' compensation. Members are expected

to make decisions in the organization's and stakeholders' best interests while complying with relevant regulations. This insurance helps protect them from lawsuits alleging improper actions or wrongdoing.

- **Meeting fees:** Some organizations pay members compensation on top of their cash retainer for their attendance at board meetings.

What Factors Affect Board Members' Pay?

The compensation that a board member receives can vary on numerous factors. Some examples include:

- **Size of the organization:** A smaller company or start-up may offer stock options as compensation because it has growth potential. If it ends up gaining significant success, it could result in large payouts for the holders. Meanwhile, large companies that earn multi-million-dollar revenues may offer cash compensation to board members.
- **Whether the organization is public or private:** Private organizations often do not compensate board members with equity. Instead, they may rely on paying them via cash retainers and meeting fees. However, a public organization can provide additional compensation in the form of equity by offering them shares in the organization.
- **Type of organization:** For-profit organizations typically offer some form of monetary compensation to their board members. However, individuals who serve on the board of a non-profit organization often perform this role on a volunteer basis. They typically do not receive salaries but may get reimbursement benefits for travel.
- **Industry:** Because there are no specific compensation requirements, payment can vary widely amongst industries.

These differences may occur due to varying industry standards or averages and responsibilities associated with the role.

- **Members' employment status:** Outside board members, or individuals external to the organization receive compensation for serving on the board. Meanwhile, inside board members, or individuals otherwise employed by the organization, do not receive additional compensation for their board role.
- **The number of meetings:** If an organization decides to pay its board members for their attendance at meetings, their payment will vary on how many meetings are held.

How to Become a Board Member

Becoming a board member can be difficult, but there are some steps you can take to help you pursue this goal. These steps include:

1. Determine your preferred board type

Take time to think about the type of board you would like to serve on, along with the role you would like to perform. Identifying your current skills and interests can help give you an idea of the type of organization that best suits you. You can also think about your career goals and what you would like to gain from serving as a board member.

You can choose whether you would prefer to serve on the board of a non-profit or for-profit organization based on your interests, experiences, and skills. The difficulty of gaining a board position may also be a factor, as it is typically easier to gain a seat at non-profits. A non-profit seat can serve as a good starting point to gain experience before seeking a corporate board role.

2. Identify and develop your professional skills

Next, examine your existing skills and experiences more closely. Boards look for members with expert knowledge in a particular area, so try to determine your niche. You can also research what skills are in demand in your industry or by specific companies. For example, many boards appreciate members with strong financial knowledge, and the areas of social media, digital transformation, cybersecurity, and data analytics artificial intelligence are a big focus in this market.

Once you identify your niche, highlight it on your resume and make an effort to continue developing and using those skills. If you do not have existing board experience, find opportunities to interact with your current company's board or serve on a local or community board. You want to demonstrate you have significant and relevant experience when meeting with board members and applying for opportunities.

3. Research companies and board members

You can find websites that publish board openings, similar to job boards. You can also reach out to specific companies directly or your contacts to inquire about potential opportunities. Companies posting board openings online will outline the types of candidates and credentials they desire, which will help you assess whether an opportunity is right for you.

If you are looking at a public company or organization that has not posted an opening, you can still research its current board members to assess your fit. You can learn whether it already has members within your niche or a knowledge gap that you could fill. You may also discover whether any members seem close to retirement, which could provide an opening soon. This research also offers networking insights.

4. Start networking

One of the most effective methods of gaining a board position is to utilize your professional network. If you already belong to an organization, connect with its board members and ask about their experience gaining board membership. They can provide helpful, specific advice, and you can demonstrate your interest in a board seat. Try to also reach out to your existing professional contacts, especially those who serve on boards, to gain more insights and learn about any potential openings.

To build your professional network, join associations relevant to your industry or profession. There are also groups aimed at board membership that host public events, such as the National Association of Corporate Directors. These groups serve as a great way to make new and potentially powerful connections. While networking, make sure to relay your interest in finding a board seat and include specific details about the type of position you seek and the skills or experiences you can offer.

5. Demonstrate your value

Whether you gain an interview for a board member position via an online posting or networking, you need to demonstrate why you deserve the opportunity. Show your interest in the specific board by researching the company, its board members, and the industry. If you can display how your existing skills and experiences align with the organization's values and mission, it can help impress its board members. You could be making decisions regarding its future, so this alignment is necessary to assure stakeholders that you will keep their best interests in mind.

If you identified a gap that you can fill, focus your discussions on those relevant skills or knowledge. For example, if the board wants to boost its cybersecurity efforts, you can demonstrate your prior experience implementing cybersecurity strategies for an employer and the ensuing positive results. Identifying the unique skills you could provide serves as an effective method of differentiating yourself from other candidates or existing board members and demonstrates your value.

How to Research a Target Company

1. Look for companies that share your values
2. Research employee benefits the company provides
3. Learn about the company's business operations
4. Research the company's leadership
5. Expand your research to news and recent events

6. Ask your network for opinions
7. Scan the news headlines for red flags
8. Set aside the time necessary to research properly
9. Review related local news stories, forums, and business journals
10. Understand the type of company you want to work for
11. Be strategic in how you share your research in an interview

1. Look for companies that share your values

Other than pay and benefits, 43% of candidates say they are attracted to a new job because of meaningful work. By researching a company's core mission, you're not only ensuring they have clear goals but ones that resonate with your interests and passions. If you value social causes, diversity initiatives, or innovation, choose a company that aligns with these. Read reviews from past and present employees covering areas like company culture, salary, job advancement, and work/life balance.

2. Research employee benefits the company provides

To attract potential employees, companies often disclose healthcare benefits and other perks, including stock options, flexible work schedules, or unique onsite facilities that may include gyms or catered cafeterias.

You can see what others are saying about benefits there, along with conversations on the hiring and interview process and company culture. You can even ask a question yourself. Also, review the *Careers* and *About Us* pages on a company's website as well as their social media channels.

3. Learn about the company's business operations

How does the company make money? Who buys their products or services, and are they highly rated? Is the company a start-up, or if it's been in business for a while, how has it grown over time? What industry is this company in? The answers to these questions will give you an idea of how stable this business is, what some of their immediate concerns might be, and how you could play a part in their success.

For public companies, you can get this information from the company website as well as access certain financial information, and office locations and learn how the company is structured. Public companies typically post annual reports and other public financial documents online. You can also consult resources like Crunchbase to learn about funding, mergers, and acquisitions, as well as the competitive landscape.

Look out for information that will help you answer questions about the industry and how the company you're researching could pull ahead or maintain its lead.

4. Research the company's leadership

When a company captures your interest, you should get to know who is leading the way. Research the employees who hold respected positions within the company by reading the "About Us" page and employee bios on the company's website. Seek out the social media profiles of executives and department directors—What are their posts like? Are they proud to represent the brand or work in this industry? Some company leaders may have been interviewed or written books and articles that give you insight into their thinking.

5. Expand your research to news and recent events

A company's website, blog, and social media are great ways to learn about a company, but you'll also want to get an external perspective. Search for general news coverage and specific industry publications for recent updates about the company and its competitors. Scanning customer forums and product reviews can also help you gauge a company's or their products' reputation.

6. Ask your network for opinions

Seek opinions from trusted, reliable friends and associates. After you've done your research, discuss what you've learned with your network. Ask people you know for the inside scoop on their own company's culture and if there are opportunities. If you're a recent college graduate building your network from scratch, ask university advisors for names of alumni working at your target companies. Consider reaching out to these people for a quick coffee.

7. Scan the news headlines for red flags

It's a good idea to scan headlines for major changes in a company's recent past. Note any significant events, such as widespread layoffs, corporate mergers or buyouts, a new CEO, etc. Such changes can bring opportunities but could also result in low employee morale and leave a volatile work environment in their wake. Proceed with caution.

8. Set aside the time necessary to research properly

It's important to note that this research does take time. If you can't set aside several hours at one time, break it up into dedicated 20-minute blocks. Dedicate each block to researching a different part of the company. Use **Google Alert** to track all news about the company and its executive team and C-Suite leaders.

9. Review related local news stories, forums, and business journals

If you're interested in working for a smaller private company, you may have difficulty tracking down information online. Fortunately, there are thousands of media sources—including national and local news, trade publications, business journals, forums, and blogs—that provide articles and product reviews. Also, try your local Chamber of Commerce offices or the Better Business Bureau.

10. Understand the type of company you want to work for

If you're a new college graduate or in a career transition, you may want to start by building a list of industries that best suit your knowledge, skills, and interests. The Bureau of Labor has compiled a comprehensive list of industries to start with. You can also explore the best companies to work for. Navigate by industry and company ratings to find a variety of organizations that will fit your new goals.

11. Be strategic in how you share your research in an interview

After learning all you can about a company, you may be tempted to showcase that newfound information during the interview. But be sure you do so strategically and to your benefit. Use the information you've learned to connect your skills and experience to the job description, goals for the department, and vision for the company throughout the interview.

Be aware that some of the information you've found may be outdated. If you've found sensitive information in your research, think carefully before bringing it up in the conversation. Creating an awkward situation with the hiring manager by attempting to show off your researching talents may backfire.

Company research is time well spent for developing knowledge of an organization, preparing for interviews (especially the favorite: *"So tell us why do you want to work here?"* and writing an eye-catching cover letter. It also helps you make an informed decision about whether a company is a good match for you.

Chapter 3

Interview Advice From a CEO

"In today's economy, Job Security is the Ability to Secure a Job!"

Mark James

From a recent survey of CEOs, here is a list of deliverables, contributions, and abilities that they look for in the ideal candidate for the executive team in their company.

The next time an employer or CEO asks or thinks to himself or herself, **"Why should I hire you?"** you need to see the question in a new light -- as an opportunity to shine and pull ahead of your competitors and get to the job offer stage.

Let's take a look at a few important factors when interviewing for your ideal position:

BE MEMORABLE – *Ask thought-provoking questions that prove you've done your homework on the company.*

Everybody wants to feel like they can make an impact. It's easy to get discouraged when you're pounding the pavement for weeks or even months. One way to make an impact right off the bat is to ask thought-provoking questions that prove you've done your homework on the company.

For example, if I owned a men's wear shop and wanted to hire a tailor, I would be much more impressed with someone who asked me about my product than someone who asked me about the benefits.

It's a good idea to make sure you know what your interviewer thinks is important for this job and company and cut out anything you don't think will add value. Of course, by asking if there are any other areas that would be valuable to explore, you may get some ideas for how else to contribute once you are hired.

Again: The more information you have ahead of time (i.e., BEFORE walking into that interview), the better prepared (and more confident) you'll feel when it comes time to make a great impression. Remember, you can never ask too many questions when going into an interview!

LISTEN TO QUESTIONS – *If you don't understand, ask for clarification.*

Don't jump in with answers until you understand the question. Clarifying questions is important for listening, understanding, and learning—they don't make you look bad. It's better to find out that you've misunderstood something than it is to do or say the wrong thing.

When asked questions, it is important to give understandable and useful answers rather than responding with some generic statements.

Sometimes, follow-up questions are the best solutions to a question you don't understand or have the answer to. If you can't answer to someone's satisfaction, don't be afraid to say, "I don't know" or "That's not my area of expertise." The CEO or interviewer expects your opinion, but they also expect your expertise and your thoughtful insights. Never be afraid to say that you aren't sure about something, and never be afraid to say that you don't know or understand. If you can find out and get back to them, do it. You might have that opportunity at a second interview.

DON'T OVERSELL – *It makes you appear anxious and desperate.*

When you oversell, you are lying. You are telling your dream as it would be in perfection, not as it really is with the bumps and bruises. Overconfidence goes along with overselling because oversellers believe they can accomplish more than reality shows them they actually can accomplish. If you oversell yourself, you need to stop it now before you oversell yourself out of a job.

Overselling implies that you overinflate the facts about yourself and your abilities. Oversellers lie to their customers. They make promises they can't keep. They overstate their results.

How can you avoid overselling? Be honest about your abilities, your accomplishments, and your limitations, then overdeliver on your promises. You will be respected more for handling yourself with honesty than for overselling and overpromising.

BE CONCISE – *Less is More; many answers are WAY TOO LONG! The Art of great communication is brevity!*

Keep it short, simple, and to the point. Listen, as opposed to talking, except when it is appropriate. Be calm, articulate, and logical. When you are asked questions, do not give a college dissertation! Elaborate as needed, but don't go overboard.

BE ACCURATE - *Don't claim credit for something you didn't do on your resume. If part of a team, say so; don't say you led the team.*

Be truthful and accurate on your resume. Don't pretend you did something you didn't do. Don't exaggerate your accomplishments to try and impress an interviewer.

Unless you really did lead a team, don't say you did. You might be hired to actually lead a team, and the first time you fail, because you don't have the experience, you'll be back out looking for another job.

Remember, facts can be checked out, so stay honest and true.

ASK GREAT QUESTIONS - What separates candidates in this CEO's mind is the quality of the questions they ask.

Receiving quality questions from job seekers is equally as important as giving quality answers during interviews. This shows that the person is truly interested in the position. It also shows that they've done their homework and come in prepared.

Questions to ask might include:

1. What's the most important quality you want in an employee?
2. What might my performance be like if I were hired?
3. Do I have any gaps in my experience?
4. What is your company culture like?
5. How do I compare to other applicants?
6. This job description is very different from my last one. Why do you think I am qualified for this job?

It is the quality of questions that really shows whether or not you should hire someone because job seekers who ask quality questions are usually those who are willing to work hard, as well as work smart.

DON'T RAMBLE - *If asked for an infomercial about your career, watch the length. For this CEO, it should be five minutes tops. (In my opinion, I would say many CEOs might prefer even shorter responses - probably less than 2 minutes MAX!)*

It's something we've all seen in interviews. The interviewer asks, "So, what was your favorite hobby when you were younger?" The interviewee goes off on a 30-minute tangent about how they once built their own racecar out of an old bicycle, several lawnmowers, and scrap metal from a run-down trailer.

It doesn't matter if you were amazing in the debate club in high school or won the basketball state championship in college. Interviews are an opportunity to get your name in front of people quickly. They're not the best place for long, drawn-out stories that have no real bearing on who you are now or what you want to do. The thing to remember is that interviews are short. Interviews are done by people with busy jobs, so you need to get your point across quickly and precisely.

If you are asked how you decreased your last company's accounts receivables, just tell them you developed a five-part system that worked, which can be instituted at any company. Don't list all five steps and explain in detail how they work. After all, they will need *you* if they are curious!

So remember, the next time you're going into an interview, ask yourself, "What can I say that will make this person want to hire me?"

SUGGESTED RESUME LENGHT – *For this group of CEOs, they suggested 2-3 pages maximum.*

The general rule is one page for every ten years of experience. However, most professionals today follow a "functional" or "skills-based" approach, in which the candidate highlights specific skills for each position.

You should take into consideration several factors when deciding on your resume length:

- What are you applying for? Different positions require different resume lengths. A resume that is too long or too short can work against you.
- How much experience do you have? The more experience you have, the shorter your resume should be. A resume with five years of experience can probably fit on two pages; ten to fifteen years of experience requires a one-page resume, and twenty or more years is normally limited to one page.
- What do you actually do? If you include all of your previous

- What do you actually do? If you include all of your previous positions, internships, and volunteer experience, the length will quickly expand. The more detailed information you provide for each position or job title, the longer it takes to read through your resume.
- Are you including an objective? If you write an objective on your resume, it will take up another line.

Be sure your resume is pertinent to the job.

BE REALISTIC - *Tough to convince him that you're open to a reduced role than where you were (he used the analogy of moving from a 4,000 square ft. home to a 2,000 square ft. home.) You can do it, but there are lots of things you'd miss! Do consider folks for reduced roles if they're* **MEMORABLE?**

Sometimes it's easier to get your foot in the door if you are open to taking on a different job than the one you are applying for. Many times employers will have several positions open. Even if you're overqualified for a position, it might be wise to say you would accept that position with a promise that when a better fit opens up, you will be considered for it.

BE VERY PREPARED - *If asked back for a second interview, you need to do even more homework – dig deeper during this conversation.*

Second interviews are equally as important as the first ones, maybe even more. This is when a company really gets to know you and see how well you fit in with them. Obviously, you've already made a good impression in the first interview, so keep the momentum going.

The best time to prepare is before you even get an offer for a second interview. That's when you want to have all of your second interview questions ready. Memorize them, practice them, do whatever you can to be completely prepared. That way, when you are asked second interview questions, it will seem like second nature for you because you've already gone over the answers so many times in your head.

Second interviews are usually a bit more casual, so it may be difficult to know when you're supposed to ask second interview questions. If the interviewer hasn't asked second interview questions and you feel your time is almost up, it's your time to shine! Take this opportunity to let them know more about yourself.

You may even be interviewed by a second manager, so many of the questions you asked at the first interview can be repeated. It's always a good idea to get a different perspective from another member of the company.

RESPECT THE TIME - *Manage your time in the interview.*

Don't ask for detailed information, feedback on how you did, tell jokes or anecdotes, etc., with only two to three minutes left. If you want feedback, let the person know earlier in the process.

Tip: Always ask for the next steps in the hiring process. What is the "Call to Action?" "Where do we go from here?" Be prepared, especially if they hint at a second interview.

LIKEABILITY – *Can I work with this individual for the next 3-5 years and enjoy the working chemistry we have established? This is usually a "gut feeling."*

Keep in mind that this interview is a two-way street. You are being interviewed to see if you can actually do the job, if you are the perfect fit for the company, how well you can get along with others and if people can work with you. However, is the job exactly what you want?

Can you work with the interviewer/CEO/Manager? Do you like or agree with the company's motto or policies? Are you willing to take a cut in pay just to have this job? Do you see yourself climbing the ladder or staying lateral in the next 3-5 years?

Just as with any relationship, it's not only if they like you. You have to like them back.

THE BIG PICTURE – *It's more than just the interview.*

You will need to be prepared to discuss the following areas of interest that the CEO wants to validate:

1. Your skills and competencies
2. Your researched knowledge of the company
3. Your value to the company
4. Your worth to the company
5. Whether you can go above and beyond your job description
6. Cultural fit with team and company employees

BOTTOM LINE - What executive hiring managers really want to know is, **"What's special or different about you?"** or **"How are you different than all the other candidates who have applied for this position?"**

With this in mind, a good way to approach your answer here is to be ready to address your best "stories and examples" that answer this question: *"What is Your Highest Best Use to an Organization?"*

Chapter 4

Plan B is the New Plan A

"The Best Way to Predict Your Future is to Create it"

Plan A is the corporate track.
Plan B is the entrepreneurial track.

I started my own business in 1999 when I was 44 years old. I was really tired of the corporate merry-go-round. I made a lot of money for other people, including all my bosses. I observed my father, who always had a side job (hobby) with a product idea to market and sell. Some worked - others not so well. But he always had a positive outlook and never gave up "his vision" of success. This inspired me to evaluate my career and take the plunge – put it all on the line and go solopreneur. I purchased a URL domain, **HireConsulting.com** and launched my consulting business, and the rest is history.

Today, 10,000 Baby Boomers retire each day, sending shockwaves through the American workforce. Filling the workforce gap will be a challenge. The ranks of Gen X and Y workers are simply not enough, while many Millennials lack the needed work experience. Now is the ideal time to start your own business. Let's take a look at the current generation demographics.

Departing Boomers Leave a Big Gap

Baby Boomers make up about one-third of today's workforce. The Boomers are a generation of 75 million, many of whom are still working. Losing 10,000 a day presents a significant drain of knowledge, experience, and wisdom for the companies that employ them. These companies need to replace these retirees and fill a significant skill gap. This issue isn't going away any time soon.

Gen X and Y are Not Big Enough to Fill the Void

At 65 million, Gen X and Y simply don't have enough people to fill the gap. The Millennials are 1.8 billion strong and have become the largest demographic in the American workplace. They are hungry for jobs but haven't yet had the opportunity to acquire the wisdom and experience they will need to lead the workforce. By 2030, Millennials will make up 70 percent of the American workforce. And although 2030 sounds far away, we'll be there in 8 short years.

Experienced Consultants Can Fill This Gap

There has never been a better time than now to jump into the workforce as a consultant. Companies are going to need specific skills and experience that they can't acquire through hiring employees. This need will continue for several years until the Boomer gap is filled. An experienced consultant, who can hit the ground running with little guidance and make an immediate contribution, is exactly what these companies will need. Roll up your sleeves and get to work. Now is your chance to be a Superhero.

Boomers (1946 – 1964)

The Baby Boomers were born from the mid-1940s to the early 1960s. Almost exactly nine months after World War II ended, "the cry of the baby was heard across the land," as historian Landon Jones later described the trend.

More babies were born in 1946 than ever before: 3.4 million, 20 percent more than in 1945. This was the beginning of the so-called "baby boom." In 1947, another 3.8 million babies were born; 3.9 million were born in 1952, and more than 4 million were born every year from 1954 until

1964 when the boom finally tapered off. By then, there were 76.4 million "Baby Boomers" in the United States. They made up almost 40 percent of the nation's population.

The Boomers grew up during a time of prosperity and great social change: rock and roll, Vietnam war protests, civil rights, women's rights, birth control pills, and the sexual revolution. Boomers are retiring at a rate of 10,000 per day, as previously noted.

Gen X and Y (1965 – 1981)

Generation X and Y follow the Baby Boomers. They were born from the mid-1960s to the early 1980s. The generational dates are not exact, so some late Boomers identify more with Generation X and Y. They grew up during a time of skyrocketing divorce rates. Many of them were latchkey kids as mothers joined the workforce. This generation grew up with a distinct lack of adult supervision. It's interesting to see that these latchkey kids have grown up to be today's helicopter parents.

Gen X and Y are often referred to as the sandwich generation because they are at a life stage when many are caring for both children and aging parents. This means not all of them are working full time. Work-life balance and flexible work are becoming critical for retaining these X and Y employees. This amplifies the Boomer gap.

Millennials (1982 – 1996)

The Millennials were born from the early 1980s to the mid-1990s. Most Millennials were between the ages of 5 and 20 when the 9/11 terrorist attacks changed the lives of all Americans. Millennials are the most racially and ethnically diverse adult generation in the nation's history. Older Millennials helped elect the first black president of the United States. Most Millennials came of age and entered the workforce during the height of the recession. It will be interesting to see how this slow start will play out over the decades as the Millennials age.

Millennials demand more flexible work schedules and measure job opportunities by more than money alone. They have a new vision for work-life balance. The side-hustle is common, so companies are going to have to work to retain Millennials.

Gen Z (1997 – present)

Gen Z is the newest generation, born between 1997 and 2012. They are currently between 9 and 24 years old (nearly 68 million in the U.S.) These kids have grown up fully immersed in the digital world. The oldest of this generation are reaching 25 years of age, with many now out of college, getting married, and starting families. Gen Z is the most racially and ethnically diverse generation of Americans yet. According to the Pew Research Center, non-Hispanic White Gen Z'ers hold a very slim majority at 52%. Hispanics make up 25% of Gen Z, while Black Gen Z'ers make up 14%, and 6% are Asian. The remaining 5% are a different race or two or more races. The majority of Gen Z members are not immigrants: Only 6% were born outside the United States.

While past generations have taken up social issues, Gen Z is more social-minded than previous generations. Gen Z'ers are focused on seven key social issues: healthcare, mental health, higher education, economic security, civic engagement, race equity, and the environment.

Let's Fill the Gap

There has never been a better time to jump into the workforce as a consultant. Keep in mind there are 5 different generations in today's workforce. We will all need to become adept at working across generations to be successful. Your teen and his grandfather may both be working as Walmart greeters. Some Boomers will continue to work well past 65, including yours truly. As a Boomer, I connect with more Boomers, Gen X and Y, and Millennials. Keep in mind to maintain relationships with Boomers who have a tremendous amount of knowledge, expertise, and wisdom to share.

3 Action Steps to Generate Revenue NOW!
By Amy Rasdal, author; Land a Consulting Project NOW!

It's easier than you think to start and build a 6-figure consulting business. All you need is a computer, a phone, brainpower, and business experience. The work is the same as the work you've been doing in your corporate job, only better.

The best way to get started as a consultant is to dive in. These three action steps will help generate revenue now. If you start right away, you can be doing billable work as soon as next week. Following these three action steps gives you the best possible chance of landing a consulting project. It works for me, and I see it work for others, over and over again. Take control and take the plunge!

Here is a brief overview of 3 Action Steps to Generate Revenue NOW!

1. Define your value proposition
- Outline your services
- Focus on the benefit to the customer
- Draft, iterate and go! 80% is good enough

2. Make your list of people to tell – must be > 100
- Everyone can come up with at least 100 people to tell

3. Tell everyone you know
- Send an email to everyone
- Then book meetings and phone calls with those people most likely to hire you now

In addition to Amy's Top 3 Actions Steps above, I have added a fourth. Strategize and develop a **"Portfolio Business"** with several revenue streams to mitigate risk and increase your upside.

4. Learn How to Develop a Business with Multiple Revenue Streams

Six Types of Entrepreneurial Track Opportunities:

1. Consulting Solutions
2. CxO Fractional Management
3. Franchise Ownership
4. Interim Management
5. Purchase a Company
6. Bootstrap a Company

Self-employment Tips:

Learn how long it takes to realistically build a sales pipeline. Ask other self-employed consultants. Solution Selling Starts with Trust – nothing else matters if the customer/client does not trust you!

Some skills can be outsourced - IT, Finance, Taxes, SEO...But it's essential to be able to sell, market, develop new business, deliver it and provide superior customer service.

Who enjoys cold calls? (No one!) Always be seeking warm calls through common referrals and introductions. Your ability to network and connect with prospects is critical. ***Your Network is Your Net Worth!***

Try Rebooting Yourself During Your Job Search: Control Alt Delete

If self-employment is not your gig, let's get back to the main thing – your job search. Do you know those times when you feel stuck? When it feels like no matter how hard we push, nothing seems to go quite right, or at least not how we wanted. When life seems to lock up at the wrong time, and it's all unplanned. What do we do when our computers or devices lock up, get overloaded, or stuck? The first method of troubleshooting: Hit

Control, Alt, Delete. Somehow, it works. And I thought about restarting in life.

Control: When I feel stuck or frustrated, I realize it's either because I'm trying to control something I shouldn't or can't; OR I'm not taking control where I need to and the "tail is wagging the dog." Let's check the control button. Do we need to let go of something we can't control, or are we trying to control too much and denying others the opportunity to step in and grow? Maybe we've been avoiding a decision, action, or conversation and it's time to step in, take control, be bold and provide proper boundaries and guidance.

Alt: After we have a firm finger on our "Ctrl" trigger, we need to hit "Alt" to alter our behavior. To get different results, we will need to alter our behavior. What behaviors can we alter to produce a different outcome? And if we truly believe our behaviors are in proper alignment, then check any "ALT-terior" (ulterior) motives. I call this checking my heart, or in other words, what are the true reasons I am doing what I'm doing. Sometimes I find my heart is not in the right place.

Delete: Now the hard part. We have to Delete the prior events or what we've been making up in our head. We have to get rid of the pent-up frustrations and stop carrying around the past. We start from now - and I mean Right Now. There is no history to remind us of anything. Most people like to say, "Live like it's your last day." I prefer "Live each day as if it's your first." See everything with a fresh new perspective, full of opportunity, excitement, and wonderment.

With Control Alt Delete - we can Restart! And there will be a pause, a blank screen for a bit and that's OK. We need to afford ourselves a little time to reboot. We all have different operating systems, so be patient.

Remember, **"Network is a VERB - Not just a NOUN!"**

66

The biggest concern for any
organization should be
when their most passionate
people become quiet.

Chapter 5

How To Hire Great Talent?

Every business leader encounters obstacles depending on their industry and their business's specific challenges. But, while each business leader holds a unique position, there are similar issues that apply across every sector.

This issue is also among the most pressing for a CEO to address if they want to ensure they are leading Talent management – Are the right people working for you?

Most CEOs are well aware of the issues they face regarding talent management. As industries have become increasingly complex, the demand for individuals who can fill vital positions has increased.

It's not just performance where talent management has become a significant concern for CEOs. There is also the importance of finding staff with the right personality to match the organization's culture.

Regardless of whether these talent management efforts are aimed internally or at external experts, finding and hiring the right people that suit your business thinking is essential.

Making this step a priority can ensure hiring and promoting the right people who fit the company culture. Great companies understand that people are their most significant asset and a significant factor for ongoing business growth.

Why You Must Follow the 'Rule of 3' to Hire Great People

I've been in the recruiting business for 25+ years. As I talk to the world's leading recruiters and the best talent leaders, it's clear that with few exceptions, there are three prerequisites to consistently hiring the best people for other than entry-level roles, specifically:

Rule One - *You must have a great job.* The best people aren't looking for lateral transfers, whether they're active or passive job-seekers. So if your job descriptions are laced with hyperbole and an excess of "must-haves," you won't have a single top performer to consider.

Rule Two - *You must have a great recruiter.* Whether they're actively looking or not, most candidates emphasize what they get on Day 1 (title, location, compensation, company) as a condition to proceed. Yet, those who do move decide to accept a job based on what they'll be doing during the first year, the team they'll be working with, and what they could become if successful. To be considered significant, recruiters need to convince great people to focus more on doing and becoming rather than opting out if what they get on Day 1 isn't overwhelming.

Rule Three - *You must have a great hiring manager.* It's commonly assumed that managers hire people just like themselves. If so, it explains why they find it challenging to hire diverse candidates or people stronger than themselves. However, the opposite effect is rarely considered: the best people want to work for the best managers. They also don't want to work for managers less competent than them. This is the likely reason managers can't hire people stronger themselves, not that they don't want the competition.

The Best People Are Not Applying to Your Postings

If you're not seeing or hiring enough strong people, you're most likely misfiring on one of the big three. Some solutions follow, but they all require an understanding of the labor market. The following survey is from over 1,500 fully-employed LinkedIn members in the U.S. and Canada.

The major findings:

- Only 23% of the fully-employed professional workforce is actively looking for another job.
- The semi-active candidates – representing 13% of the workforce – silently seek other positions through a close network of associates.
- The most significant segment of the talent market – the semi-passives at 43% – are not looking for another job. However, they would entertain a call from a recruiter if the job represented a significant career move.
- The super passives, at 21% of the talent market, don't even want to consider changing jobs. However, if you can somehow connect with them and describe an extraordinary career move, they might be willing to discuss it.

With this segmentation of the labor pool, here are some ideas on how to attract everyone:

- **Offer great jobs** by banishing traditional job descriptions that list required skills and describe lateral transfers. This is a pretty simple one to try out. Just describe the actual work people will be doing and prepare compelling ads and email messages based on this. Here's an article on how to do this, here's a legal discussion on why this complies, and here's an example of a career-oriented job posting. If you want to test this idea out, here's a video describing a simple proof of concept. The idea: compare two sets of candidates on quality – those who can do the work and are excited by it to those who have all of the skills.
- **Hire a great recruiter** who can find and attract people who aren't looking. A great recruiter has to do more than screen active candidates who apply. It's safe to assume that there are more top people in the 77% of those who are not actively looking.

Recruiters need to find the best people in this group and convince them to consider your open job. Of course, to hire these great people, the job must be a great movie, not just a bunch of glowing statements with little substance.

- **Become a great manager**, or at least fake it. The Gallup Group has made a big thing about their Q12 list of factors that drive employee satisfaction and performance. At the top of the list is clarifying job expectations upfront. This alone will allow you to craft a great job. Most of the rest revolve around the hiring manager's role in supporting and developing the people in their group. So get the book, and follow the steps. Not only will you be considered a great manager as a result, but you'll also be seeing and hiring more substantial people.

Following the "Rule of 3" is not easy. It takes commitment, discipline, and the desire to hire the best person for every job. However, the rewards for the manager, the recruiter involved, the company, and especially the person hired is nothing short of remarkable.

Conducting Objective Interviews

It's been demonstrated that 70% of the hiring assessment can be affected by first impressions and whether the candidate and interviewer get along. However, personality in the interview doesn't predict performance, nor is it an accurate indicator of actual nature. Some candidates are temporarily nervous; others are socially outgoing and are on their best behavior. More errors are made in the first 30 minutes of the interview than any other time. Many great candidates have been excluded too early because the hiring manager didn't follow these simple steps. Accurate hiring assessment takes reprogramming.

10 Great Reprogramming Techniques

1. Wait 30 minutes before making any decision - Recognize when you feel relaxed or uncomfortable. Fight to keep the buying switch in the "maybe" position. This way, all information has equal value.

2. Conduct a 20-minute phone interview before you meet them in person - when you talk to someone on the phone first, you automatically minimize the impact of personality and first impressions.

3. Don't start the interview right away. Go on a tour, see a demo, but get into a give and take discussion. This will help minimize emotions and set up the framework for a good dialogue.

4. Ask all candidates the same questions, regardless of your first impression. Write down a few **Performance-Oriented** questions to ask right away.

5. Measure your first impressions again after 30 minutes - Revisit the first impressions. Compare them with your original assessment and evaluate your reaction. This will help restore balance.

6. Change your frame of reference. If you like the person, be skeptical and ask more challenging questions. If you don't like the person, give them the benefit of the doubt and ask more straightforward questions.

7. Listen four times more than you talk - the interview is not a casual conversation. It needs to be a fact-finding expedition. You can accurately determine the candidate's competency with a **4 Question Interview.** *(below)*

8. Treat the candidate as a consultant or a valued customer - We always listen more to experts or have a superior position. Treat candidates the same way to elicit more open responses.

9. Talk about real work - Discuss problems and related business issues. Accuracy will increase if the interview is more like a problem-solving session than an inquisition.

10. Use panel interviews. You will save time if all decision-makers are present. There can be no disputes on what was answered and discussed, which minimizes the scheduling of multiple individual interviews.

Top 4 Employer Interview Questions

A recent survey shows company executives lack interviewing skills.

The survey was conducted by sending questionnaires to 195 CEOs in mid-size companies, with 35% responding. The survey reports that 96% of executives said it is "essential" to select employees who fit their organization's culture, values, and mission. Yet only 17% of those executives claimed: "a great deal" of training in selection interview techniques. While companies say human resources are the key to success, many are weak at the selection process's critical point- the interview. There are still too many managers who think a chat over lunch will let them divine the talents of a candidate and the emotional and psychological ambitions of a candidate.

The interview is not a casual conversation. It needs to be a fact-finding expedition. You can accurately determine the candidate's competency with the following eight questions:

Question 1 – (Opening) Create an exciting position:
(Describe an overview of the company and work and major objectives, then ask:) Can you give me a quick overview of how your background and experience have prepared you for this leadership position?

Question 2 – Determine the trend of personal accomplishments and energy: (Ask this question for the past 2 – 3 jobs)
Describe a quick overview of your (current/prior) position, and can you describe the most significant impact (change) you made or when you took the initiative? Spend the next 5-10 minutes of fact-finding to get a clear understanding of the process used to achieve the results. Ask this same question for the past 2 to 3 positions to see the trend of personal accomplishments over time.

Question 3 – Determine the trend of team leadership:
(Ask this question for the past 2 – 3 jobs)

How would you describe your organization (draw an organization chart) and how did you develop and manage your team? (or tell me about some team project and describe your role). (Spend 5-10 minutes on fact-finding. Ask this same question for the past 2-3 positions to see the trend of team leadership.)

Question 4 – Anchor – Determine the comparability of past accomplishments:
(Ask for each SMART objective) One of our key performance objectives is _____ (describe objective). What is your most similar past accomplishment?

Question 5 – Visualization – Determine the ability to adapt and anticipate the needs of the position:
(Ask for just the top 2 objectives]

If you were to get this job, how would you go about implementing and organizing the _____ (describe performance objective) ?

(Get into a 'give and take' discussion with the candidate about real issues.)

Question 6 – Commitment, character, and values:
Can you tell me about a time you were committed to a task?

(Do fact-finding to understand better the real accomplishment and how the candidate went the extra mile)

Question 7 – Personality and cultural fit:
What three or four adjectives best describe your personality? Give me examples of when these have aided in the performance of your job and when they have hurt. (Compare this personality to your 1st impression. Also, look for honesty and self-awareness.)

Question 8 – Create supply and express your interest in the candidate:
Although we're seeing some other acceptable candidates, I think you have a solid background. We'll get back to you in a few days, but what

are your thoughts now about this position? (Don't go too fast. Make the job worth earning. Create a competition to test genuine interest.)

Notes:

ANCHOR - From an employer's point of view, it <u>should</u> be essential to get a past comparable accomplishment to determine a candidate's ability to achieve a critical **SMART** objective.

SMART - **S**pecific, **M**easurable, **A**ction-oriented, **R**esult-based, **T**ime-bound Example: "Within six months, improved factory production by 3%."

VISUALIZE - Determine the candidate's competency and ability to anticipate and understand the performance requirements of the position. Well-prepared candidates should know their most significant **SMART** accomplishments *and* relate **how** they would achieve your critical objective.

Past performance is a strong predictor of future performance. The candidate's ability to **ANCHOR** and **VISUALIZE** during an interview is a strong predictor of success.

What Is the Real Purpose of the Interview?

Is the real purpose of the interview to weed out the weak or attract the best? Too many people, including a good chunk of corporate recruiters and hiring managers, view the interview primarily as a means to disqualify people. In the process, they miss a golden opportunity to attract stronger candidates, demonstrate the company's professionalism, overcome errors made by weaker interviewers, and most importantly, hire top people who are more interested in career growth opportunities rather than significant compensation increases. The primary purpose of the interview is to assess competency, or is there more to it? Since my 25-year stint as an independent third-party recruiter always involved the hard-to-find, hard to attract, and hard-to-hire types of candidates, I have some preconceived notions. The big one: assessing competency is essential but not sufficient, and if you're going to do it at all, you might as well do it right.

The Four Big Purposes of a Professional Employment Interview

1. Accurately assess competency, fit, and motivation. According to the research report cited above, a primary interview requires the following:

- ✓ **Structure:** You need to ask everyone the same questions in a logical order that minimizes the impact of biases and extracts the correct information.
- ✓ **A Job Analysis:** you need to know what job you're trying to fill if you want to determine if someone is competent and motivated to do it. (BIG NOTE: a skills-based job description is NOT a job analysis. A job analysis describes the work the person needs to do on the job.)
- ✓ **A formal rating and assessment scale:** Specific guidance is needed to convert answers into a quantitative performance-based assessment.

2. Prevent good candidates from being improperly assessed. If you're a recruiter, you've experienced this problem first-hand many times. It happens whenever a fully-vetted candidate you've worked hard to find gets blown out because the hiring manager conducted a superficial or flawed assessment. If you've ever been on the interviewing team, you've experienced the problem second-hand. This happens whenever there is a wide disagreement about candidate competency among the interviewing team members. It means most interviewers use emotion, intuition, or some narrow range of factors to determine competency, fit, and motivation to do the work. One countermeasure for this type of incorrect assessment is specific evidence disproving the false conclusion. For example, assuming that a soft-spoken person lacks team skills can be debunked by describing the big, multi-functional teams the person has been assigned to and asked to lead.

3. Clarify real job needs, and demonstrate to the candidate that the assessment is professional and the company has high hiring standards. Candidates – especially those with multiple opportunities – react negatively to box-checking, overt selling, superficial assessments, and interviewers who are clueless when asked, "What's the focus of the job, and what are some of the challenges the person hired will face right away?" Conducting an in-depth performance-based interview using the Most Significant Accomplishment question eliminates these concerns. This structured approach clarifies real job expectations (the #1 driver of performance and job satisfaction). It ensures the candidate fully appreciates the importance of the job, that they were adequately evaluated, and that the company has high hiring standards.

4. Shift the decision to career growth rather than compensation maximization. Long ago, I discovered that there was never enough money in the compensation budget to attract top performers. So I gave up trying. Now I use the interview to figure out a big enough gap between actual job requirements and what the candidate has already accomplished. If this "career gap" (e.g., bigger team, bigger budget, better projects, more impact and exposure, faster growth, etc.) is big enough, compensation becomes less critical. If the gap is too wide, the candidate is too light for the job, and if the hole is too small or nonexistent, the job isn't big enough.

Bottom line: If you have more than enough top candidates to choose from, you increase your chances to hire the best people, which is the ultimate purpose of the interview.

Chapter 6

Behavior Assessments: Pro vs. Con

Why Employers Use Job Interview Assessments

Job interview assessments and tests are specifically designed to evaluate and measure your capabilities to determine how well you fit the role you are applying for. They give an idea of your potential and the likelihood of success in the job. Assessments can be specific to a role; for example, you might be assessed on your grammar and editing skills if you apply for an editor position. However, you might also be evaluated to determine personal characteristics such as extroversion/introversion or your potential to demonstrate behaviors valued by the company, such as teamwork, leadership, and problem-solving abilities.

The success of an organization lies in the competence of its employees. Highly skilled employees are innovative, efficient, and productive and thus can bring exponential success to an organization. Traditional methods solely used during the hiring process, such as scanning resumes and face-to-face interviews, offered limited insights into a candidate's potential to succeed. Performance on interview tests is a much more effective recruitment tool, as they specifically evaluate a candidate's ability to fulfill the job requirements and their potential for long-term success.

Job interview test scores are reliable indicators of a candidate's performance on the job and likelihood of retention by an organization. Employers also use these scores to compare the performance of several well-qualified and experienced candidates to determine the ideal candidate for a role. This helps to streamline the hiring process, identify top talent, make successful decisions faster, lower the risk of wrong decisions, lower employee turnover rate, and enhance the quality of the recruitment process.

To obtain a holistic overview of your capabilities, you might be asked to take several on-site or off-site types of tests. Besides your aptitude and skills that measure your ability to learn and succeed in playing a specific role, some tests can assess your needs, drives, personality, and behaviors. The ultimate goal is to understand your potential to fit in a company's culture.

Myers-Briggs and DiSC are the two most well-known names. But in the HR community, The Predictive Index (PI) is well known and respected.

The Predictive Index (PI) Behavioral Assessment is an untimed, free-choice, stimulus-response tool that is far more than a personality test. For more than 60 years, thousands of businesses around the globe have used the EFPA-certified PI Behavioral Assessment. This allows companies to understand the personality traits and what makes employees and candidates tick.

The Team Discovery tool is like the Swiss Army knife of assessments. It's very versatile for the different tools available to utilize with the behavior assessment that PI has produced as a survey. PI works, and it also helps discover how teams interact with each other. It only takes six to ten minutes to do online. It's a beautiful tool that yields great reports, helps people chart their career development, points out strengths and cautions, and has excellent coaching tips.

How Predictive Index Can Help Organizations

PI also goes beyond helping to reduce bias in hiring, promoting, and succession planning. Further benefits of PI that helps your organization include:

- Increased hiring and talent selection from the 50/50 flip of a coin to 80-90% in hiring accuracy.
- Determines Hi-Performing employees who are deemed promotable and ideal leadership development.
- Understands teamwork styles so you can use natural strengths and coaching to build high-performing teams.
- Builds relationships, improves internal communication, and expands emotional intelligence to solve people's problems fast.
- Unlocks strategies and builds your capability to coach your direct reports.
- Isolates and improves low employee engagement, improve employee retention, and increases revenues.

Eliminating Bias and Increasing Diversity in The Hiring Process

Many organizations are starting to understand the benefits of diversity, equity, and inclusion (DEI) in the workplace and it's important to their current and prospective employees.

Unintended biases can very easily be present in any organization's hiring practices. The way someone crafts a job posting, the weight someone gives to certain elements of a resume like education — these factors can influence who gets an interview and who doesn't, and who gets hired and who doesn't. But do they actually help organizations obtain the right candidate for the position?

Selecting candidates to move forward, based on education and experience, can exclude viable candidates because certain minority groups haven't historically had high levels of access to education and job experience compared to other candidates (e.g., women compared to men, people of color compared to white individuals, disabled individuals compared to abled individuals). At the end of the day, if someone chooses to move forward with candidates based on education and experience and thereby excludes diverse candidates, they are hurting their organization's ability to evolve. And the evolution brought about by innovation is necessary to surpass the competition, gain market share and meet the future needs of customers.

Plus, by better aligning candidates to a position, you can help reduce costly turnover. How many times have you seen a newly hired employee quit a few weeks in because it turned out the job wasn't a great fit for them after all? Behavioral drives and needs are much more important to job fit and job satisfaction than you might have thought.

6 Most Common Types of Tests You Can Face During an Interview

Employers use assessment tests to evaluate your aptitude, personality, skills, and ability to perform tasks during the recruitment process. Assessment tests help determine your suitability for a role, as they are a better indicator of your preparedness than previous experiences and accomplishments. The following are common types of interview assessments and tests, how you can prepare for them, and why employers use them:

1. Aptitude or Psychometric Tests

These tests evaluate specific skills such as logic, reasoning, numeracy, verbal ability, and problem-solving that you are likely to use during your work. As aptitude tests are strictly timed and usually completed within 30 minutes, they show how well you can think, process information, and work under pressure. Employers use a variety of testing formats (paper-based or online) to assess your aptitude for a specific role. Typically, these are multiple-choice tests with only one correct answer. Employers have specific benchmark scores to compare the performance of several candidates for a particular role.

Types of Aptitude Tests
- Numerical Reasoning: Determines your ability to deal with numbers and interpret numerical data such as averages,

percentages, ratios, etc., including analyzing and drawing conclusions from tables and graphs.

- Verbal Reasoning: Determines your ability to understand language, comprehend written passages, and make deductions.
- Abstract Reasoning: Determines your ability to identify and interpret non-numerical and non-verbal patterns.
- Logical Reasoning: Determines your ability to think logically, such as identifying sequences, recognizing patterns or relationships between shapes and imagery, and non-verbal skills, such as identifying analogies and structures.
- Diagrammatic Reasoning: Determines your ability to interpret diagrams and flowcharts logically.
- Inductive Reasoning: Determines your ability to solve problems by identifying patterns and analyzing data when faced with unfamiliar information.
- Situational Judgment: Determines your ability to think critically and make decisions and judgments when encountering specific workplace situations.

How to Prepare

- Ask prospective employers for the type of aptitude test you have to take and the test format. Then, practice strictly under test conditions. For example, if you have to take a paper-based test, practice on paper, not online.
- Identify the areas in which you perform poorly. Focus on improving on these.
- Although you can never know the exact questions you could be asked, if you are familiar with the various types of questions and practice under time constraints, you can do an excellent job on the actual test.

How to Ace Aptitude Tests

- Sleep well the night before your test, as your mind will be clear the following day.
- Eat something before the test and stay hydrated.

- Avoid distractions, especially if you are taking the test at home.
- Be mindful of the time allotted to complete the test during your exam.
- Read and understand every question carefully. Follow the instructions.
- Focus and concentrate on your test.
- Take a few deep breaths to think clearly.
- Move on if you get stuck rather than struggle with a specific question. Leave a challenging question and complete the others.
- Return to unanswered questions if you have time in the end.
- Be fast, but do not rush.

2. Personality and Behavior Assessments

These tests assess beliefs, communication style, work ethic, interpersonal, teamwork, leadership skills, and how you respond to various situations. Importantly, they help employers determine if your character traits are suited for a specific role and the likelihood that you will enjoy and succeed in that position in the long run. For example, an assessment may determine if you will succeed in a sales job without prior experience. If a job role is not a good fit for your personality, it could lower engagement, productivity, and satisfaction.

Most Common Personality and Behavior Assessments

- **Predictive Index Behavior Assessment (PI):** Full disclaimer; I am a Certified Partner with The Predictive Index and this behavior assessment sets the benchmark. It provides multiple tools, such as talent selection and optimization, leadership development, team discovery, employee retention, and improved employee communication. Note: The PI is not a Test – It's a survey. The PI Behavioral Assessment is an untimed, free-choice, stimulus-response tool far more than a personality test. Companies use the PI Behavioral Assessment to hire candidates who are a great fit for the job requirements. PI helps companies design teams

62

that perform and communicate more effectively, and to manage employees in a way that pushes them to achieve and perform at the top of their game. The PI results report is divided into four personality factors: **A – Dominance B – Social Interaction C – Pace/Patience D – Formality.**

- **Myers-Briggs Type Inventory (MBTI):** Determines your inclination to one of the two traits in the groups "Extroversion (E) vs. Introversion (I)," "Intuition (N) vs. Sensing (S)," "Thinking (T) vs. Feeling (F)," and "Judging (J) vs. Perceiving (P)." Depending on your preference, you can have one of 16 possible personality types. For example, you can be an INTJ (introversion, intuition, thinking, and judging). The test format consists of 93 questions. There will be two sentences for each question. You have to choose the sentence that best describes you. MBTI can show how you take in information, make decisions, work, and communicate.

- **DiSC Behavior Inventory (DiSC):** Determines your dominant traits based on four personality types: "Dominant (D)," "Influential (I)," "Steady (S)," and "Conscientiousness (C)." It is much shorter than other tests, with only 12–30 questions. You will be presented with statements such as "I am very daring" or "I find it difficult to relax." You have to choose one description that applies to you the most and another that applies to you the least. Companies commonly use diSC to determine your professional behavior, work style, and ability to work on a team.

- **The Caliper Profile:** Determines how your personality characteristics correlate with your ability to perform a role. The test consists of 180 multiple-choice questions. It can be in either a paper-based or online format. You must answer all questions. There is no time limit; applicants need 2–3 hours on average to answer all questions. This test cannot be scored if you leave any question blank, so answer every question. The questions can be in several different formats. For most questions, you have to choose one statement that best or least describes your views and beliefs.

- **Hogan Personality Inventory (HPI):** Evaluate your personality and determine a good fit for a specific role. Administered online and scored instantaneously, it consists of seven primary scales, six occupational scales, and 42 subscales. There are 206 true/false questions, with a 15–20 minutes completion time.

- **The SHL Occupational Personality Questionnaire:** Determines how your personality characteristics can influence your performance and long-term potential for a specific role. There are 104 questions; although untimed, it takes 25–40 minutes to complete. Each question consists of four statements, and you have to choose one statement that best and least describes you.

How to Prepare

As personality tests do not measure your knowledge or skills, you do not need to study or prepare for them. But, if you are eager to know how you will perform on an actual test, you can get sample questions that will give you a better idea of the nature of these tests. This will also give you insights into specific traits that you could work to improve or use to your advantage.

You can prepare for the Caliper Assessment. Besides questions to assess your personality, such as True/False questions and "five degrees of agreement" with "strongly agree" to "strongly disagree" responses, there will also be questions on pattern recognition and abstract reasoning, like in aptitude tests. Suppose you are applying for a specific role, research to determine the ideal Caliper profile for that job, and practice. Know the critical competencies for a specific role—for example, interpersonal skills for communications jobs.

How to Ace Personality Tests
1) Take time to understand the question.
2) Be honest and genuine, as there are no right or wrong answers.

3. Specific Skills Tests

These tests determine if you have skills specific to a highly specialized role. For example, knowledge of specific programming languages for IT roles or your ability to edit or write for editor or writer roles.

How to Prepare
- Identify the skills that are required for a specific role.
- Ask employers for the test format and duration.
- Practice diligently under time constraints.

4. Job Simulation Tests

These determine how you will perform in actual work settings. Formats can vary and include in-person, take-home, online assignments, presentations, or role-playing.

Presentations

These assess your communication skills, public speaking, analytic and persuasive skills, creativity, and ability to convey the needed information in the allotted time. Presentations typically last 15–20 minutes. Microsoft PowerPoint is the most common software used by many companies.

How to Ace Presentation Tests
- Be calm, and avoid fidgeting.
- Speak in a relaxed, audible tone and pace.
- Maintain eye contact.
- Emphasize important points.
- Ensure you complete on time.

5. Written Tests

You will have to write an essay or report or review or summarize a published or unpublished document, generally on word processing software, such as Microsoft Word.

How To Ace Written Tests

- Follow directions carefully.
- Define abbreviations at first mention.
- Structure and organize your content by grouping similar ideas together.
- Ensure the flow of ideas.
- Be careful of spelling and grammar.

6. Group Activity Tests

These assess communication, enthusiasm, teamwork, leadership, and problem-solving skills as part of a team:

- Discussion/Case studies: You have to discuss a business case or scenario and express your views
- Role-play: You have to play a specific role

How To Ace Group Activity Tests

- Be active.
- Be clear and confident while communicating.
- Follow directions carefully.
- Brainstorm and build on ideas.
- Identify patterns or inconsistencies.
- Be mindful of the time.

Disadvantages of Behavior Assessments

Behavior assessments allow us to look at how individuals go about their work and achieve their objectives. Two people may achieve their objectives, but one may have used more positive behaviors than the other (e.g., organizing their time more effectively; interacting with others in a considerate manner).

Behavioral assessments are tools from the field of psychology that are used for observing, describing, explaining, and predicting behavior. Behavioral assessments are now being used outside the clinical settings, too, especially in educational and corporate sectors, considering their insightful and predictive nature.

Although there are many great points to working with behavior assessments, there are also a few drawbacks:

- ➢ Causes the person to have anxiety.
- ➢ Observer bias- not getting accurate information.
- ➢ Psychologists want to form their own impressions.
- ➢ Time-consuming.
- ➢ Difficult to compare results because each interview is unique.

So, remember to be mindful of both the pros and cons when applying these assessments.

human resources

[H - R]   *noun*

---

the unofficial lawyer, psychologist, event planner, teacher, organizer, peacemaker, mediator, facilitator, team builder, detective, enforcer, and diplomat, with a never-ending quest to hire great talent.

Chapter 7

How to Embrace Human Resources During the Hiring Process

Human Resource Management, or HRM, is the practice of managing people to achieve better performance. It's about optimizing company performance through better management of human resources. Human Resources are all the people that, in one capacity or another, work for or contribute to an organization. These individuals can be (full or part-time) employees, contractors, freelancers, interim, or fractional.

The Human Resources department is essentially responsible for five primary corporate directives:

1. Facilitate the hiring process of new employees
2. Enforce company policy
3. Mitigate employee conflict and wrongdoing
4. Avoid employee discrimination and lawsuits
5. Maintain and manage compensation and salary equity

Understanding the Seven HR Basics

When we talk about Human Resource Management, several elements are considered cornerstones for effective HR policies. These cornerstones are:

1. Recruitment, Talent Selection, Assessment, and Facilitation of the Hiring Process
2. Performance Management
3. Learning & Development

4. Succession planning
5. Compensation and benefits
6. Human Resources Information Systems
7. HR data and analytics

1. Recruitment, Talent Selection, Assessment, and Facilitating the Hiring Process

Recruitment and selection are arguably the most visible elements of HR. We all remember our first interview, right? Recruiting candidates and selecting the best ones to come and work for the company is a key HR responsibility. People are the lifeblood of the organization, and finding the best fit is a key task. The request for new hires usually starts when a new job is created, or an existing job opens up. The direct manager then sends the job description to HR, and HR starts recruiting candidates. In this process, HR can use different selection instruments to find the best person to do the work. These include interviews, different assessments, reference checks, and other recruitment methods. Sometimes, when there are a lot of candidates, HR may deploy preselection tools. These tools help to separate the wheat from the chaff when it comes to suitable candidates. The successful candidates then continue to the next round, where they are interviewed and receive a more in-depth assessment.

2. Performance Management

Once employees are on board, performance management becomes important. Performance management is the second HR basic. It involves helping people to become their best selves at work, boosting the company's bottom line.

Usually, employees have a defined set of responsibilities that they need to take care of. Performance management is a structure that enables employees to get feedback on their performance – to reach their best performance.

Examples are formal one-on-one performance reviews, 360-degree feedback instruments that also take into account the evaluation of peers, clients, and other relations, and more informal feedback. Usually, companies work with an annual performance management cycle, which involves planning, monitoring, reviewing, and rewarding employee performance. The outcome of this process enables the categorization of employees into high vs. low performers and high vs. low potentials.

Successful performance management is very much a shared responsibility between HR and management, where usually the direct manager is in the lead and HR supports. Good performance management is crucial. Employees who are empowered to their full potential improve the efficiency, sustainability, and profit margin of a business. Employees who consistently underperform may not be a good fit for their role or the company culture. These employees may need to be let go.

3. Training, Learning, and Leadership Development
People are the product of life experiences, the country and era they grow up in, and a range of cultural influences. Within HR, learning and development ensure that employees adapt to changes in processes, technology, and societal or legal shifts.

Learning and development help employees to reskill and upskill. Learning & Development (L&D) is led by HR, and good policies can be very helpful in advancing the organization towards its long-term goals.

Many organizations have pre-defined budgets for L&D efforts. This budget is then distributed amongst employees, with trainees, future leaders, and other high potentials often receiving more training opportunities than others. Individuals may arrive at a company with vastly different knowledge and experience. L&D provides employees with a way in which to bridge skill gaps and develop into leaders. A well-known framework that connects performance management with L&D

activities is the 9-Box grid. Based on people's performance and potential ratings, the HR department, together with managers, can advise different development plans.

4. Succession Planning

Succession planning is the process of planning contingencies in case key employees leave the company. If, for example, a crucial senior manager quits his/her job, having a replacement ready will guarantee continuity and can save the company significant money. Succession planning is often based on performance ratings and L&D efforts. This results in the creation of a talent pipeline. This is a pool of candidates who are qualified and ready to fill (senior) positions in case of someone leaves. Building and nurturing this pipeline is key to good people management.

5. Compensation and Benefits

Another one of the HR basics is compensation and benefits. Fair compensation is key in motivating and retaining employees. One of the fundamentals of human resource management concerning pay is ensuring equity and fairness.

Making the right offer of pay is a key part of attracting the best talent. This must be balanced with the budget and profit margins of the company. HR should monitor pay increases and set standards of merit. HR may also carry out a pay audit on occasions.

Compensation comprises primary compensation and secondary compensation. Primary compensation involves directly paid money for work, which often is a monthly salary and sometimes performance-based pay.

Secondary benefits are all non-monetary rewards. This can include extra holidays, flexible working times, day-care, pensions, a company car and laptop, and much more.

The goal here is to reward people in ways that motivate them.

6. Human Resource Information System

The last two HR basics are not HR practices but tools to do HR better. The first is the Human Resource Information System, or HRIS. An HRIS supports all the cornerstones we discussed above. For example, for recruitment and selection, HR professionals often use an Applicant Tracking System, or ATS, to keep track of applicants and hires.

For performance management, a performance management system is used to keep track of individual goals and put in performance ratings. In L&D, a Learning Management System (LMS) is used for the distribution of content internally, and other HR systems are used to keep track of budgets and training approvals. Compensation specialists often use a payroll system, and there are also digital tools that enable effective succession planning. All these functionalities can often be done in one single system – the HRIS. Sometimes, however, the management of these functionalities is split up into different HR systems. The bottom line here is that there is a significant digital element to working in HR, which is why the HRIS is the final element when we talk about the HR basics.

7. HR Data and Analytics

The last of the HR fundamentals revolves around data and analytics. In the last half-decade, HR has made a major leap towards becoming more data-driven.

The Human Resource Information Systems we just discussed is essentially a data-entry system. The data in these systems can be used to make better and more informed decisions. An easy way to keep track of critical data is through HR metrics or HR KPIs. These are specific measurements that answer how a company is doing on a given measurement. This is referred to as HR reporting. This reporting focuses on the current and past state of the organization. Using HR analytics, HR can also make predictions. Examples include workforce needs, employee turnover intention, the impact of the (recruitment) candidate experience on customer satisfaction, and many others.

By actively measuring and looking at this data, HR can make more data-driven decisions. These decisions are often more objective, which makes it easier to find management support for these decisions.

Conclusion

You now know the 7 Human Resource Management basics. None of these HR fundamentals are isolated. They all interact and affect each other. Think of these 7 basics as building blocks – strong management of each fundamental element contributes to the strength of the next. Collectively, these HR fundamentals enable a workforce not only to perform better but to perform at its very best.

What to Expect During an HR Interview

Screening interviews with human resources professionals are a crucial step to getting the job. A good or bad interview with HR will determine how far you go in the interviewing process, so it's best to know what to expect and go in prepared. As a career coach, I have worked with job candidates on how to answer the most common questions asked by HR. My mock interviews place clients in situations similar to ones they will actually face and prepare them to ace their interviews and land the job. I have always said, "The right employer won't care how long you've been in your current role if you're the right candidate."

Let's take a look at the five most common questions asked by HR during screening interviews and how you should approach them:

1. Why are you interested in this position?

HR professionals love this question, so use it as your chance to reiterate your strengths and highlight your applicable skill set and passion for the company and the role. Speak to how your past experiences match the qualifications for the job using keywords from the job description to make the connection stronger. By clearly linking your skills to the position, you are helping the HR manager envision you in the role.

Sample Answer: Having worked within the financial services sector for five years, I have gained an appreciation for the power of client-facing roles in terms of my professional development and organizational impact. As a relationship manager in your firm, I envision bringing my ability to resourcefully optimize any given client's portfolio as the best way I can help your company's five-year strategic goal of retaining its client base at a 50% rate. I have done this in the past while working for my previous employer, and I am confident that I can help you accelerate your current goals while growing my career.

2. Tell me about yourself.

As an age-old prompt that will likely never go away, it's important to know how to provide a compelling answer for an HR manager. Instead of the typical chronological progression of your background, I recommend doing a SWOT analysis within the context of a professional interview. Analyze the sector, the company, and the job function using a SWOT and look for opportunities to market yourself. I go into this in more detail in my blog post on how to tell your professional story in a way that will entice an interviewer to hire you.

Sample Answer: I have been a sales manager for X years, with experiences that include being able to lead a sales force toward the accomplishment of aggressive goals. While at Company X, I created the gold standard incentive program that resulted in helping us sell-in potential charge volume that exceeded our goals by 20% in both travel expenses and daily expenses. Prior to that, I worked at X, where I completed X, etc. Side note: figure out the critical deliverables of the hiring firm or its essential needs. Then tailor your response accordingly.

3. Why are you leaving your current job?

HR managers will ask this question to determine if there are any red flags related to your departure. Are you leaving on good terms or bad? Are you looking to escape from your current job or grow within a new one? These are a few of the questions running through the interviewer's mind. Take this opportunity to speak positively of your current employer but communicate that you're looking at this new position as the next step in your career. By framing your answer positively, you're making the interviewer focus on your potential contributions rather than any red flags.

Sample Answer: My business unit started with 50 full-time employees, and today it has 10. While this reduction in personnel enabled me to showcase my ability to produce results with limited resources in an organization where management has turned over, I am interested in transitioning to an organization like yours where there is growth potential. For example, in my current role, I managed to acquire 100K clients with only one other sales manager and a dwindling budget. In your company, I would be managing a team of 20 sales managers, where I stand to make a significant impact not only for your firm but on the firm's market share.

4. What do you know about the company?

This is a test and one you should be able to pass easily. Doing research on a company prior to an interview is a necessity. You need to know the history and makeup of the company, who the key players are, recent accomplishments and mentions in the press, and any other relevant information. Communicate the positive information you learned about the company, from awards to new product launches, to demonstrate your knowledge.

Sample Answer: Your firm competes with firm A, firm B, and firm C in the U.S. My understanding is that you are better positioned in this area vs. firms A, B, or C. Meanwhile, firms B and C bring these strengths to the table. Given my skill set, I know that I can help you optimize your strength in this and offset the strengths that firms B and C plan to invest more heavily in during 2014. *Side note: the point is to be specific in how you'd use this information to drive results.

5. What questions do you have for me?

ALWAYS have questions for the interviewer. The strongest candidates show their enthusiasm and position themselves as potentially valuable team members by asking smart, strategic questions that benefit both the interviewer and the interviewee.

The Ideal Candidate

A group of 50 HR Vice Presidents and Directors were discussing the characteristics they look for in the **"Ideal"** candidate for their firms.

The group discussion took on the following questions:

➢ What are the **"Characteristics"** you look for in candidates?
➢ What are some **"Red Flags"** to look out for?
➢ If you had an ideal **"Wish List"** for candidates, what would it entail?

The group came back with some very insightful answers. Here are the results:

IDEAL CHARACTERISTICS:

- Cultural fit to the company
- Strong (and proven) communication skills – Asks good questions, listens, and responds well
- Can show initiative, enthusiasm, and confidence
- Strong Team Player
- Exhibits humility and not arrogance or cockiness
- Strong set of technical and management skills for the position they are looking to fill

- Willingness to accept responsibility and be accountable. Don't look to place blame on others
- Shows the ability to be adaptable and flexible, and resourceful
- Has a pattern of continued learning throughout their career
- AND most importantly, "Passion" for the direction of where they are going or want to go!

RED FLAGS:

- Watch non-verbal cues during interviews and interactions. They often reveal the "true" message and/or feelings of candidates.
- Someone who is not prepared for the interview, the position or knowledge of the company.
- Someone who is arrogant and/or is not a "hands-on" person
- Makes negative and/or derogatory comments about former employers
- Inconsistent on answers to questions or information on resume
- Shows no passion for what they do or in the opportunity they are seeking

IDEAL WISH LIST:

- Someone who exhibits "active listening" during the entire interview process
- Has a customer focus both internally and externally
- Has a skill set of "people skills" of empathy, passion, and development
- Looks to move the organization forward regardless of the "level" of their role
- Has a solid career vision for themselves
- Leads a balanced life with their work
- And the #1 Ideal Wish List item --- Has a proven track record of ***Integrity, Honesty, and Ethics.***

Chapter 8

Keys to Salary Negotiation

Before you say "Yes" and accept a job offer, know these:

Your particular needs for choosing the right company. What are your passions? What are the lessons that you've learned? What are your accomplishments, which are story examples, and what are your needs? What are your needs? The needs are people, challenge, balance, and worth. Those are the four criteria to rank to determine whether or not this is the right company for you to go to work with, accept their job offer and join that company.

People are important. That always has to be number one. You have to really like them. They have to like you. You have to be able to learn from them. They have to be able to learn from you. You want to be inspired by these people. You want to know they've got vision. They're all on board. If you're the sharpest arrow in the quiver, it's going to be a long, long ride. You are not going to like it very well if you're the sharpest arrow in the quiver or the sharpest needle in the quill, and they're all looking up to you for the answers, and you're around a lot of people that are just lost. You are not going to like that job, and you're going to be looking for a new job in six months or less. There is also no chance for you to grow there.

I always say it's got to be the most challenging type of opportunity for you to really want to get out of bed in the morning because your bank account does not get you out of bed. Your balance in your checking account does not get you to not hit the snooze alarm. It's the motivation. It's the challenge, the charge, the "can't wait to do this and make a difference in the world," that you really got to love what you're doing to get out of bed in the morning. **Money is a stimulator. Not a motivator.** This is a fact. When offers are being done, offers are not there to motivate people to accept the job and go to work. The money is put on the table to stimulate them to accept it. Then the negotiation is a whole different thing, but people challenge and then balance. Balance is work-life balance. No mystery here. Some people want to work to live. Some people live to work. Know this before you say yes.

Does your plan sit well with the company? Some companies expect 70 hours a week, like a New York law firm, and then others want you to go home after 40 hours. If you're a soccer Saturday mom or dad and you've got to be up and taking kids to soccer games or picking them up after school, well, your work-life balance is different than the guy that's an empty nester or the lady, the mom, that's no longer managing a family, where they can jump on a plane tomorrow morning to Albany, New York and be happy doing it without causing trauma in the family.

Work-life balance is an important state of affairs you need to know before saying yes. That changes as we all mature and grow older and our kids grow up and raise families of their own. Ask yourself, "Is it going to be disruptive in your life?" Are you going to be able to embrace the company and do what they need you to do? In fact, there are statistics that show 50% of the people that take the first job offer that comes their way, when they're out of work, 50% of the time they're looking for a new job in six months because they jumped too soon. They ignored the red flags and the yellow flags because they just wanted to get back in the ranks and get a payroll. They jumped too soon. They settled for less, and now they're regretting it.

Then the final criteria, which is always going to be number four, is can they afford to pay you what you're worth based on your contribution? People, challenge, balance, and worth, and when you get into negotiations, it's a whole other chapter there. You definitely want to have the negotiations while the offer is still on the table. How you respond to the first offer and the whole negotiation process also matters.

The 5 things everyone wants from their job... but you can only get 3 consistently.

Here are five criteria for job happiness. The catch is that you will probably only be able to achieve 3 of these consistently in your "ideal" job. Which three are the most important to you? Which 2 are you willing to sacrifice?

1. **Live where you work**
2. **Love who you work with**
3. **Love what you do**
4. **Work reasonable hours**
5. **Make good money**

Criteria Notes:

1. Are you willing to get on a plane every week, week in and week out to do what you love? Do you hate to commute but are fine with being on an airplane to travel for work? Then you don't need to live where you work vs. someone who hates driving for 1 hour to work for a job.

2 and 3. "Love" is intentional in these two criteria. Not like, not enjoy, but really **love.**

4. "Reasonable hours" are how you define it. If you love what you do, 60+hours per week may be reasonable.

5. "Good money" is how you define it. You may work for the Forestry Service, earn $50K per year, and think you're overpaid. Or you may work on Wall Street and earn $1M per year, and it's never enough.

Negotiate the Optimum Salary Package

For years I have coached many executives through successful negotiations like the dialogue examples below. To make it even easier, I've broken it down into four easy-to-follow steps.

Step One: Try to Delay the Salary Topic

Note: In some states, it is now illegal to ask what your prior salary was. But, just in case you are asked what your salary requirements are by an HR Manager or Hiring Manager (HM), try to delay the conversation until the offer is made. If they ask you your salary requirements during the interview or on a phone screen, say something like this:

"My number one priority now is to learn more about your organization and this role to determine if I'm the best match for your needs. Should an offer be extended, I'd be happy to negotiate with you at that time, and I'm confident we'll be able to reach an agreement."

This usually takes the conversation away from salary. However, if they insist on talking about it at that point, ask them to disclose the company's range first.

Step Two: Find the Salary Range for Your Role

Why find the range? Well, you don't want to offer something too high and make the employer think they can't afford you. On the other hand, you don't want to offer something too low and miss out on a larger paycheck for yourself.

It's best to handle this by saying something along these lines:

"I'd be happy to negotiate with you. First, I'd like to have an idea of what the company has budgeted so I can negotiate within that range. What salary range is the company looking at?"

Saying this will ensure you can make a proper offer that is fair to both parties.

Step Three: Make a Ranged Offer

When you do disclose your offer, always give them a range and not a specific number. Come prepared with a range to quote. That range should be something that you know is realistic for that position and that you would be comfortable accepting if they offered you. You can find baseline information on <u>Glassdoor</u> and <u>Salary</u> if you are unsure.

Step Four: Know Your Comfort Zone

Always have your ideal number and your "deal-breaker" number that you will not accept. When you are accepting a position that pays less than you currently make, you can handle this by saying:

"Of course, compensation is important, but it's not my only priority right now. I'm more concerned about finding a position that I can enjoy and grow in. If an offer is extended, I'm confident that we can reach a fair agreement on a salary that works for both parties."

This helps keep the dialogue open for when it comes time to negotiate fully.

Executive Negotiating Statements

What do you say when you are asked for your salary requirements? Remember, the company needs to make an offer for you to evaluate it - --- Not the other way around! Know your numbers in advance. Determine what do you really **NEED** and what you really **WANT?**

Your (demands=requirements) responses could be any of or a combination of the following:

- *"I think salary is a very important topic, and I would be more than happy to discuss it once a mutual interest has been established."* (Get back to discussing your accomplishments)
- *"Your company has a very good reputation, and. I am sure the compensation package will be fair enough to keep me motivated and productive. By the way, what is the base salary range for this*

position?"

- *By the way, what is the salary range for this position?"*
- *"Based on my accomplishments and contributions, I would like to be paid at the same level as other executives of my tenure and caliber."* And ask, *"What is the salary range for a person of my caliber?"*
- *"Regarding compensation, I am flexible and willing to negotiate once we have developed a mutual interest."* (Get back to discussing your accomplishments)
- *"If we decide that I am the right person for this job, I am sure we will be able to come to an agreement on compensation."* (Get back to discussing your accomplishments)
- *"At this time, I am most interested in determining if I am the right person for this job. If there's a fit, I'm sure salary won't be an issue."* (Get back to discussing your accomplishments)
- *"Are you making me an offer? If so, what salary range did you have in mind?"* Only use this response later in the process.

Second and/or Final Round Negotiations

Go back to the Hiring Manager (not Human Resources) and say:

- *"This is a great opportunity, and I am excited about working with you (or) joining your company."*

- *"I am inclined to accept your offer; however, there are 3 (or more) items I want to discuss (negotiate) with you."*

- *"If we can reach an agreement on these items, I will be prepared to accept your offer today."* Remember, if you ask for something and receive it – you need to give something in return. That's how deals are made.

- Always try to conduct this negotiation "in person" if possible!

- 80% of the outcome of your salary negotiations will be determined by

your optimistic attitude and accurate assumptions!
• Remember, everything is negotiable, and get everything in writing!

Job Offer Checklist *(More on this in Chapter 12)*

1. Job Title

2. Position reports to

3. Start Date

4. Salary (monthly or bi-monthly pay periods)

5. Performance Review Date
   - 6-month early review?

6. Commission structure

7. Bonus
   - Eligibility? % Company Performance vs. Individual Performance
   - Possible for a pro-rate bonus for a portion of the first year?
   - Guarantee a portion of the first year's bonus

8. Signing bonus
   - Verbally indicate it is to make up for lost bonus/stock options, etc.

9. Vacation weeks /Paid Time off / Maternity leave
   - Extra weeks rather than a higher base?

10. Health Insurance
    - Effective date
    - Monthly Premiums/Co-Pay/Annual deductible

11. Retirement: Matching 401K

12. Stock options, Profit Sharing, Equity

13. Company Car or Monthly Allowance

14. Travel and entertainment expenses

15. Club membership

16. Executive Coaching

14. Relocation Expenses
    - Temporary housing
    - # of trips home
    - House hunting trip(s) with spouse
    - Real estate fees
      a) selling end - pickup 5% - 7% commission? Points?
      b) buying end - closing costs
    - Packing & moving household goods
    - Discretionary amount for miscellaneous expenses
    - Gross-up taxes

15. Trailing Spouse Career Transition Coaching Assistance

16. Separation/termination Agreement
    - 6-12 months full salary and family health benefits

17. Employment Offer/Acceptance Contingencies
    - Drug Test/Physical exam
    - Verification of college degree
    - Employment References
    - Background Check
    - Financial Credit checks
    - Behavior assessments

18. Offer Letter reviewed by an employment attorney

5 Salary Negotiation Tips that Work!

Once you've proven yourself well qualified for a job during the interview process, you have to start asking yourself the tough questions. Do you have a strong desire to work for this company? What if they don't offer quite as much money as you'd like? Is there a way to ask for a higher salary without alienating the employer?

It's normal to feel anxious or nervous. But you can learn effective negotiating skills that will help you get what you want, need, and deserve in terms of compensation.

1. Understand Benchmarking

You don't want to waste your valuable time on a company that is never going to pay you what you're worth. This means you need to understand how employers decide their salary levels and adjust your job search accordingly. Companies use a variety of benchmarking tools. These include comparing pay rates with:

- Average pay at other companies in their industry
- Average pay for professionals with your level of experience and education
- Average pay for professionals in your field in their area of the country

Most employers who are interested in great talent will be in the upper quartile of their market when it comes to pay. However, employers have also figured out that paying significantly more than their competitors actually doesn't motivate employees to stay over the long term. So, don't expect to be able to negotiate for significantly higher pay than the norm – no matter how qualified you are.

2. Wait for It...

There's an old saying, "The first person to bring up money loses." Starting a discussion about salary prematurely sends a signal that you don't place a high priority on being a good fit for a company's culture – you just care about the almighty dollar. In the same way, if a recruiter brings up money right off the bat, it's a good idea to smoothly change the subject so you can fully demonstrate your qualifications before talking about your salary requirements.

3. Negotiate Performance Pay

An employer who really wants to hire you but has limited resources may offer a lowball figure with the excuse, "This is what we can afford right now." If you want the job, ask if they would be open to discussing a performance-based bonus. You could start by saying, "Let's talk about specific, measurable results that would improve your bottom line and increase my earnings." Get any incentive pay agreements in writing during the hiring stage, so your employer is committed to following through.

4. Don't Just Talk Cash
Any discussion of salary should be about your total compensation. If the recruiter isn't familiar with the dollar value of the benefits package the company is offering, you might ask to talk with their benefits specialist. Remember to negotiate for non-cash perks that might bridge the gap between your asking price and the employer's offer.

5. Walkthrough It in Training
One of the best ways to prepare is by practicing. Pick a career coach who can prep you by role-playing an entire interview including the salary negotiation phase. This process gives you the confidence to talk money with a potential employer without being afraid you are getting it wrong.

L.U.C.K. =
"Learning Under Correct Knowledge"
Mark James

Chapter 9

Where Are All the Hidden Jobs?

Can you raed this? Olny 55 plepoe out of 100 can.

I cdnuolt blveiee that I cluod aulaclty uesdnatnrd what I was rdanieg. The phaonmneal pweor of the hmuan mnid, aoccdrnig to a rscheearch at Cmabrigde Uinervtisy, it dseno't mtaetr in what oerdr the ltteres in a word are, the olny iproamtnt tihng is that the frsit and last ltteer be in the rghit pclae. The rset can be a taotl mses and you can still raed it whotuit a pboerlm. This is bcuseae the huamn mnid deos not raed ervey lteter by istlef, but the word as a wlohe. Jsut oepn yuor eeys and you can see taht jbos are not rlaley hdeidn!

Yes, it's still a tough job market for some people, but don't despair. There is hope. Sometimes all you need are some fresh ideas, an energy boost, or a nudge in a different direction to add some extra oomph to your efforts. I hope the following advice will inspire you to keep the momentum going for what you want in your job search or career change. As you may have heard somewhere along the way, "Where there is a will, there is a way" or "You make your own luck." I have always said, "**L.U.C.K.** stands for **L**aboring (or **L**earning) **U**nder **C**orrect **K**nowledge!"

Here are ten places where you may succeed in finding hidden jobs:

1. Do an informational interview. These are especially useful when you are changing careers and breaking into a new industry. Informational interviews are not the place where you are interviewing for a job. Instead, they are where you gather valuable information that can lead you to some great referrals to people who are hiring or new resources for your current or future job searches.

When setting up informational interviews, find someone to talk to based on your interests and what you are targeting. Consider a particular job function/role, or specific industries and companies.

Use your networking (more on this in a minute) skills to request that someone agree to be "interviewed" by you for information. Schedule these meetings in person, by phone, or through LinkedIn. Prepare questions you will want to ask in advance and keep three objectives in mind. Try to connect with the person you are interviewing—research the field, industry, job function—to gain advice about your job search plan or next steps.

Some good core questions to ask in your interviews are:

- Please tell me a bit about your background. How did you get your start in the industry?
- What do you like best and least about the industry or your company and your role?
- What advice do you have for someone trying to get into the _____industry?
- Given my background, what could I do short term to make myself a stronger candidate?
- Could you recommend other colleagues I could talk to within the company or industry?
- Do you mind if I keep in touch with you periodically for advice?

Essential "to-dos" are:

- Draw on people you know to recommend people they know in your targeted areas.
- Call on your work or school colleagues, family or friends, professors, and others in your "network." Contact those people to request an info interview.
- Be polite, engaging, and brief when contacting them. Let them know who referred you. Tell them that you heard they would be

a valuable resource for information and that you are learning more about the industry/company/job function and hope they can share some advice.

- Send a copy of your resume to familiarize them with your background.
- An in-person meeting in their office is best, but you can also offer to take them out for coffee, meet them in an airport lounge, suggest giving them a tour if they are stopping in your city, or even do a phone meeting or IM session.

2. Get by with a bit of help from your friends. Networking is an outdated word. Today, new age networking is about building a great base of diverse relationships in which you both give help to others and receive it over time. It's about expanding your circle of friends and colleagues you can draw on as career connections. Building your relationships means conducting ongoing actions every day, such as:

- Making a point to meet three new people at your work-related functions (conferences, tradeshows, training, etc.)
- Volunteering for at least one good cause a year (a food kitchen, community event, school function, etc.)
- Engaging with the people around you while browsing in a bookstore, waiting in line at the supermarket checkout, and attending your aerobics or yoga class. Yes, talk to strangers, but rely on your excellent instincts to be selective.
- At your partner's work event, get to know the other partners, what they do, and where they work.
- Getting involved in your professional or a particular interest group.

3. Create your job. If you see an unmet, enormous need, move to fill it! If there are many small companies that you see need certain kinds of services and you have the experience to do it, then productize it and offer it. If you are a frequent flyer and see that all airlines could benefit from a certain kind of online survey, then come up with something and test it out. If you are complimented on your ability to pull an outfit together or to entertain or plan events, then why not start with one or more clients and build from there through positive word of mouth. The possibilities are endless but are bound by your financial situation and risk profile.

Creating your job means filling a need. It is providing a product or service that is valuable and that others are willing to pay for. This can be a big idea or a small one. Think about the origins of eBay, Amazon.com, or the field of sports agents.

4. Go back to the future. Embrace your past. Go back to it and draw on it to move you forward in your future. Who were the managers, the colleagues, the executives in your past work experiences who impressed you? Were there some you thought were cool or those you truly enjoyed being around? Did someone wow you so much that you tried to emulate them? Reconnect with those people. Many will have moved to different organizations. This is a good thing because it means a broader network of connections.

Your former colleagues may not have specific jobs for you but may prove to be a font of information for areas in their companies that are or will be hiring. Or, at minimum, they can tell you which companies in their industry are doing well and growing. They can also guide you to companies that have the kind of executive teams and cultures that resonate with your own set of values. Going back to the future also means that you may go back to work for a previous employer. People there know your track record. If you did not burn your bridges when you left, they would be more likely to give you some flexibility to try something new—a new job in a different group—that is aligned with your current interests.

5. Be true to your school. There is something uniquely special about contributing -- giving back -- to your school, especially when there is a beautiful community of people and culture that fits your values.

Schools always enjoy their alumni involvement. Many MBA programs also hire many of their alumni for key roles within the school—career management, admissions, and alumni relations, to name a few.

Explore how you can use your strengths to contribute to the community. Start by doing your homework on the school website if you have not kept up with what's going on. Get a feel for the current state of the school, its top priorities, any significant changes with changes in deans, and the types of ongoing or future initiatives that could leverage your talents.

Call an administrator or professor—someone you were close to—to get the scoop and ask for advice on which areas might be most receptive to you and ideas for whom to talk. For example, connect with those you know in the career center, admissions, alumni relations, or corporate relations. If it's finance, accounting, or HR you are interested in—all schools have these areas, but you may need to start with someone you know in another group and be referred to those areas.

Call on them if you had a good relationship with the dean or associate deans. Be transparent about your genuine interest in contributing to the school and ask what specific opportunities may fit now or later. Fill them in on your background and have some thoughts on where you think you might be able to make the most difference. For example, if you've been on the fundraising committee, perhaps a role in development is an option. Since school, if you've been working in high tech, maybe something related to their e-commerce initiatives, including e-learning or IT, would be feasible. If you've been involved with admissions information sessions or interviews for school applicants, maybe admissions are right up your alley. If you have managed to get through five different jobs and bounce back from a lay-off, your experience could help the career management center.

6. Make it like the Matrix. Make cyberspace work for you. More than 3,000 Internet sites are related to work, employment, jobs, and careers. They are not created equal, however, so use your time wisely. Research them, focus, and choose discriminatingly the two to five that will work for you. Post your resume on sites that offer high-quality job opportunities in the specific industries and functions that you are targeting. Use the option to have "matches" with your preferences emailed to you if that is available. Three of my favorite sites are WetFeet.com, Futurestep.com, and careerbuilder.com. (Check out my article Career-Related Websites for MBAs and Other A-List Talent for more top sites.)

7. Play sleuth. Who are growing companies? Which company is doing well, despite the lousy economy? What companies have filed numerous patents? Who is expanding internationally? Which is still hiring or posting jobs on their websites or participating in career fairs? Come up with a top-ten list of companies that match what you want. Visit their websites and look up their employment opportunities. Network in through anyone you know who can help get you in the door to talk with someone. Branch and build from there with your persistence and enthusiasm. If you see no one, then take a chance and write to the CEO or one of your alumni.

8. Contact someone you admire. Has someone recently spoken at your school who inspired you? Have you been to a conference and been impressed with a panelist or session leader? Did you meet someone who was an extraordinary person at reception or social events? Are there alumni from your school (undergraduate, MBA, or even high school) who you have admired from afar? Write to them and genuinely tell them why you admire them (without gushing). Let them know up front that you would appreciate their advice and wisdom on your career aspirations.

See if they will talk with you or ask some questions via email. Give them some brief, compelling points about your background/experience so they get a feel for who you are and what you've done.

9. Get physical. Enjoy the great outdoors when you can. It'll energize you as well as balance all of the intellectual and emotional energy you've been putting out for your job search. Go swimming or fishing, walk your dog in the park, play a basketball or beach volleyball game, or invite a group of friends to a baseball game. Ask your friends to bring their friends—at least two others that you do not know, and you've instantly expanded your circle of potential career connections. Or better yet, volunteer or inquire about job opportunities that allow you to be outside and physical. Working at the zoo, park, community center, or YMCA, or building a home with Habitat for Humanity are some options. Others are being a cruise ship activity director, stage manager for plays in the park, or walking tour guide of your historic downtown area.

10. Play host and facilitate. Start a book club or career action group. For a book club, focus the books on career- or job-related topics. Use the last ten minutes to share ideas and contacts on jobs. Also, rely on the group members to give and receive moral support. At the start, let people update the group on how the job search is going and get advice for any problems.

Everything you need to know about the Hidden Job Market

The Hidden Job Market is Not Hidden!

- Hidden jobs are hidden only from those who have their heads stuck in the internet job listings.
- Hidden jobs are right next door at your neighbor's house.
- Hidden Jobs are at the Church you go to.
- Hidden Jobs are the people sitting next to you OR right across the table from you when chatting with your friends and family.

- Hidden Jobs are at Trade Shows, Conferences, Chambers, Chapter Associations, Vacation Trips, etc.
- Hidden Jobs are at EVERY Networking Event – (Online or Live in-person)
- Hidden Jobs are on your Cell Phone.
- Hidden Jobs are in your Email Contacts.
- Hidden Jobs are in LinkedIn Groups.
- Hidden Jobs are the existing contacts in your LinkedIn Connections.

What is this elusive "Hidden Job Market?"

It is simply a non-published, little-known collection of openings and opportunities that only insiders, owners, company officers, board members, and C-suite executives know about.

The key is, how do you get to know about any of these hidden jobs?

Or maybe the key is this: how do you get the insiders to know about YOU, what you want, and how you are the right person for the job?

The hidden job market is right in front of you, but you don't know it, and because of poor personal branding and poor networking, it doesn't find you!

You can try as hard as you want to find the job seeker silver bullet, but it all comes back to defining your brand, creating and executing a job search marketing plan, and becoming a master at networking.

Top 10 tips for Uncovering the Hidden Job Market

Step 1: Give Up the Job Seeker Label

Step 2: Get to Know Yourself - Adopt a New Empowering Identity

Step 3: Develop Advocates that can Refer You

Step 4: Translate Your Accomplishments into Solutions and Value

Step 5: Have a Great Resume and Create a Special Report or White Paper

Step 6: Develop and Use a Powerful Letter of Introduction

Step 7: Use Social Media Strategies to Identify Matching Problems and Needs at your Target Companies

Step 8: Conduct Conversations with People Matching Your Profile (Peer-level networking interviews)

Step 9: Complete Profitable Agreements with the Best Organization(s)

Step 10: Utilize an Effective Learning and Career Management Coaching System to Keep You Focused and Accountable and Ensure and Accelerate Your Success.

Networking Works!

Networking: it's something that we all know we should be doing, but there's a reason that networking comes up so frequently in career discussions - it works! No matter what stage of your career you're in, whether you're looking for a new job or are happy in your current organization, networking is a handy tool that can, and should, be practiced by just about everyone.

Most people associate networking with a job search while looking for a new job as an excellent reason to leverage your career network and build new connections with others in your industry. Networking has many other benefits that can prove helpful at any point in your career. The most effective networking is done consistently, over time - not just when you're in a position where you need help. Remember, networking is the #1 way to find hidden jobs!

*"The networking event you choose **NOT** to attend - could be the next great job lead you will **NEVER** get!"* Mark James

Top Reasons to Network - *It Can Help You Find Your Next Job*

When it comes to looking for a new job, the single most impactful thing to do to increase your chances of success - is networking. Many organizations do not advertise open positions, so having contacts in your industry - or a field you're interested in entering - who might be able to tell you about relevant roles is critical. Connections in your network can also provide valuable entry points to big companies by giving you a referral or directly connecting you with a hiring manager.

It Will Set You Up For Future Growth

One of the big mistakes people make when networking is viewing it as something only done when looking for a new job. While networking can be one of the most significant factors in a job search, it's just as important to do it while you're not looking for new work. The reason? Building your career network slowly and sustainably over time will help you have the resources you need in place when and if a time comes that you do want to make a job or career change. Starting early on and continuing to nurture your network throughout your career means that you'll have a robust group of connections to reach out to when you need to - and if you've cultivated those relationships effectively, they'll think positively of you and won't hesitate to lend a hand.

It Will Give You a Network of Resources

People tend to forget that having a robust career network of talented individuals in your field can be an essential resource for the work you do on a day-to-day basis. Networking works when you focus on a challenging project and need advice on a particular aspect. When you are trying to fill a role on your team, are looking for feedback on potential vendors, or need someone with a different skill set to collaborate with, you can - and should - look to people in your network for help.

It Will Help You Grow as a Professional

An underrated benefit of networking is that it can help you grow as a professional, mainly by helping you find mentorship opportunities. There is so much to learn from seasoned professionals in your field who have built careers you admire, and most of them are more than willing to share their perspectives, give you advice, and help you develop professionally. Having one or more mentors is an essential part of growing your career. Suppose you identify someone who could be a potential mentor to you and cultivate a genuine relationship with them. In that case, chances are they'll be invested in your success and can offer much-needed guidance as someone who has "seen it all."

It Will Help You Meet New People and Expand your Contacts

Although networking is primarily career-oriented, it's also about connecting with people who have something in common with you. Sometimes that's a shared field or industry. Still, often it's something broader: an interest in promoting a certain kind of mission across workplaces (for example, sustainability or diversity), belonging to a specific group of people (such as being a woman or minority in a particular industry or being a young professional or being affiliated with the same institution, such as a college alumni network. Building relationships with these individuals might not help you get ahead career-wise (although you never know what might come of these connections). Still, it will help you meet people that you might not otherwise get to know and broaden both your personal and professional perspectives.

It's Easier Than Ever

When people think of networking, they often picture walking into a big event with a stack of business cards and having to make small talk with strangers. While there are still many networking events like this - and some people prefer them - many people would rather network on their own time, in lower-pressure scenarios. Many online networking platforms have been created over the past few years, allowing folks to network digitally. These networking sites can be cross-industry (such as LinkedIn) or specific to certain groups or institutions and offer a way to stay connected - and connect with new people - in a digital format.

The Secret Formula for Networking Success

Over the years, I have discovered that marketing is powered by two things: Know-how and a Nurtured Network of Contacts. That's it. That's the secret!

HC x SC x R = NS *(Codified Formula)*

The codified formula for **Networking Success** (NS) is based on your **Human Capital** (HC - *what you know*) times your **Social Capital** (SC - *who knows you*) times your **Reputation** (R - *who trusts you and what they say about you*)

Having knowledge, good business relationships, and a solid reputation, plus social capital and trust is the ultimate security blanket in good times and bad. Today's economic conditions present an excellent time to increase your market share by reaching out and building better relationships with people you already know. Increasing your social capital is not about sitting alone in front of your computer trying to come up with a winning marketing formula on your own. No one I know who is successful does it that way. Get out from behind your computer and meet with real people – **face to face**!

Successful people may have started out going it alone, but as soon as they possibly could, they began to leverage their own and other people's ideas, experiences, and relationships, and that's what it's all about.

*"The difference between **Not Working** and **Networking** is **ONE** Letter!"*

Chapter 10

Job Security Is the Ability to Secure A Job

EQ Vs. IQ

When it comes to your career, having a high IQ (Intelligence Quotient) is no longer enough—EQ (Emotional Quotient) plays a much more critical role today. In this chapter, I will talk about optimizing your executive EQ.

Of course, if you have both, that's a gift, but at any rate, I encourage you to think about your EQ and how you can make it a priority every single day. It will serve you well in life, I promise.

EQ is like a tennis game—between you, yourself, and the people you communicate with daily. It's never-ending and needs constant care and maintenance.

EQ is a lifetime challenge because it involves dealing with your own emotions but understanding and adapting to the feelings of others. To improve your EQ, you have to constantly be aware of how you come across different scenarios and understand who your audience is to elicit the best response from them.

Reading other people's emotions and being socially aware enough to tailor your communications accordingly is a huge thing to do and a skill like no other.

Another way to look at Executive EQ is "relationship management." This analogy brings to light the importance of improving your EQ.

Suppose you can improve your Executive EQ and master how to develop and maintain good relationships, communicate clearly, inspire and influence others, work well in a team, and manage conflict. In that case, your personal and professional connections will flourish.

The first step to optimizing your Executive EQ is being conscious of your own emotions so that you can identify them and pinpoint their root cause.

Once you're mindful of how you arrived at a specific emotion, you can work your way to the required emotional state and take your stakeholders along with you, which allows you to communicate more effectively and develop stronger relationships.

Possessing a high Executive EQ means:

- **Being aware that emotions can drive our behavior and impact people (positively and negatively)**
- **Learning how to manage emotions—both our own and others—especially when we are under pressure**

Building Blocks to Improve Your Executive EQ

In a nutshell, the key skills for improving your Executive EQ, and your ability to manage emotions and connect with others, are:

- **Self-awareness**
- **Self-management**
- **Social awareness**
- **Relationship management**

When you're ready to improve your Executive EQ, ask yourself a couple of questions:

1. Do you pay any attention to your emotions?
2. Do you have a good relationship with them?

If you can't answer these both with a resounding **"YES",** then you need to start looking in the mirror and making a change. Your career will thank you for it!

Stay Out of Job Interview Limbo

Most of the time, there seems to be an endless wait between a job interview and the next step in the hiring process. Often (but not always), they are confused because they didn't ask how the employers' processes worked, so they get discouraged and give up or, worse, they put their whole job search on hold, waiting to hear back from an employer. Don't make those mistakes!

Understanding the job, the organization, and the people you would be working with is critical to guide you in accepting—or rejecting—a job opportunity. The answers to these key job interview questions will keep you on track and informed about what is happening on the employer's side of the situation.

Here are several important job interview questions to selectively ask the HM (Hiring Manager) about "The Interview Process" before, during, and after your job interviews:

1. **Ask: What is the next step in their hiring process?**
2. **Ask: How soon do they need to fill the position?**
3. **Ask: When will they be back in touch? (Who calls who?)**
4. **Ask: What is the best way to reach your contact?**
5. **Ask: When can you get back in touch with them?**
6. **Ask: Has anything changed since we last talked?**

Final Thoughts: While some employers will tell you about their process, many will forget or just not keep you informed. It's up to you to gather the information about each employer's hiring process to gauge your chances of landing the job or not?

Top 5 Reasons You Never Hear Back After Applying for A Job

People often wonder why they never hear anything back after they hit 'send' on the email with a resume attached or on the online job application. If you're very lucky, you might have a preliminary email exchange with a recruiter and then never hear from them again. It's a depressing experience and one which also casts a shadow on the hiring company's reputation. So why does it happen? Is it you, is it them, or is it just something every candidate must prepare for in the hiring process?

Many HR managers and recruiters complain that as many as 50 percent of people applying for a given job simply aren't qualified. Adding to the challenge, most large companies – and many smaller ones – use talent-management software to screen resumes, weeding out up to 50 percent of applicants before a human even looks at a resume or cover letter. The deck is definitely stacked against the job seeker. So how do you break through and get noticed?

Stop Applying for Jobs Online!

If you want to get hired, you need to talk with an actual hiring manager. If that's a vice president or COO, so be it. Find out who this person is before you send your resume anywhere. You can locate the names of these people through various sources, including the company LinkedIn, the company website's About Us/Management Team page, phoning the company receptionist or customer service to inquire, or researching the business online using Google, ThomasNet.com, or Lead411 or Reference USA with your local library card.

Never call human resources or an in-house recruiter. These people have no vested interest in talking with you. In fact, they don't want to talk to you. You'll only foul up their daily process.

In short, your job search is just that: **Your** job search. Take control, and drive the process yourself. Work through your contacts to get internal and external target company referrals and introductions to Hiring Authority Management. (Not HR)

Don't play by others' rules, putting your future in the hands of people who offer to pass around your resume. Get into the driver's seat and make their phone ring with a follow-up call every time you send a resume or introductory letter.

Here are my top 5 reasons you're not hearing back after applying for a job, with five suggestions for ways to avoid the Resume Black Hole:

Why You Never Hear Back:

1. **You really aren't qualified.** If a job description specifies a software developer with 3-5 years of experience and you're a recent graduate with one internship, it's unlikely you'll get a call. Avoid disappointment – don't apply for jobs for which you lack qualifications. Most job descriptions are written with very specific requirements. Yes, the company is trying to find the most qualified candidate; yes, they are trying to weed people out. It's not personal; it's business.

2. **You haven't keyword-optimized your resume or application.** Job descriptions are salted with keywords specific to the skills or attributes the company seeks in applicants. A close read of the job description is a necessity, as is keyword-optimizing your resume and cover letter if you're using one or email. If the job description lists words in a certain order, e.g., a list of programming languages required, use the same order in your resume.

3. **Your resume isn't formatted properly.** You might think distinctive formatting will set your resume apart, but automated programs don't care if a document is pretty. Be consistent when formatting. When in doubt – hire a professional resume writer.

4. **Your resume is substantially different from your LinkedIn profile.** It is critical to make sure they match what's on your resume. This may seem to be a contradiction – in #1, I advised keyword optimization – but it's really common sense. Jobs worked, employers, years on the job, and other details should match.

5. **The company received 500 resumes for one job posting, and yours was 499th in.** Looking for a job is a full-time job. Do your research – know which companies you want to work for, organizations where you sense culture fit. Create a search agent to notify you by email (ExecuNet and RiteSite provide this tool) when a job has been posted that meets your criteria. Being early with your resume or application does matter. Check back in the first few days to make sure the listing hasn't changed. Often a company will post a job and, halfway through the process, change the description. It's hard to game the system. Your best bet is still a personal referral, and even that may not be enough to get a call. So, what can you do?

Remember, you need to simply STOP being a job applicant!

Here is How to Get Noticed:

1. **Research interesting companies on social media.** Find out who the recruiters are and follow them. Many will tweet new postings, so watch their streams and jump on anything for which you are qualified. And if they tweet news saying the company's had a great quarter, retweet the news with a positive comment.

2. **Consider starting a blog in your area of interest or expertise.** It's a social world; time to build a trail of breadcrumbs leading to you. Include the blog and links to any especially relevant posts in your emails to recruiters with whom you're working.

3. **Get professional help with your resume.** A professional resume writer can help you increase your odds of getting more attention

with a great resume and getting through the talent management software to the decision-makers.

4. **If at all possible, don't wait until you're out of work to find your next job.** I realize for many people this isn't possible or might even be offensive, but your chances of finding the next job are best when you're still employed. Learn how to manage your career proactively. Consider hiring a reputable career coach to guide you through this career transition management process.

5. **Network! Network! Network!** Old advice, but still true. Be visible, be upbeat, and be informed about industry trends and news in your area of expertise.

The Golden Rule of Networking:

"People will do business with and network with and refer people in their network to those people they know, like and trust and respect."

#1 Seek out warm referrals from the people you know, like, trust, and respect.

#2 Always be trying to schedule a face-to-face meeting with the warm referrals you are given by the people in your network. Once you have been given a warm referral, force yourself to make the phone call within **48 hours** to start your networking connection and secure a meeting. Then follow up and follow through!

Finding a job is tough, no question about it. I've talked to other recruiters who say they only respond to 30 percent of applicants. The odds are good you'll be in the 60+ percent who hears nothing a lot of the time. Don't take it personally – it's not a rejection of you; it's a reflection of the times. If you don't hear back, know you're not alone. Just move on to the next target...and let it go!

How to Handle Multiple Job Offers

What **ONE** thing would you either add to or subtract from each offer to make it the ideal job? Often the response is immediate, clear, and unclouded by all of the other factors in the decision-making matrix. For example, "take away the commute, and it's a done deal.

Here are the two recommendations for reaching the right decision when faced with multiple job offers:

1) Refer back to your initial job search goal and professional objective and determine if your current opportunities meet your criteria objectives and/or how each offer compares. Now make a T-List of pros and cons for each scenario.

2) Next, try to "pretend" as if you accepted offer #1 for a 24-hour period and imagine how it feels. Remember to gauge the Top 4 Decision Making Criteria: 1) People 2) Challenge 3) Balance and 4) $Worth. Then, for the next 24-hour period, "pretend" you have accepted offer #2 and see how that feels. This will often allow objections to come to the forefront, or conversely, will generate a level of excitement that the decision becomes clearer.

How to Make the Right Decision Every Time

When a job seeker is compelled to make a decision on whether he or she wants to work for a new company and accept an offer of employment, many different reasons (good and bad) come to mind. When faced with this all-important career decision, the best way to address this process is to break your decision into four critical sub-parts.

Here are the Top 4 Criteria to make the right decision every time:

1. **PEOPLE** – When deciding to work for a new company, it is all about the people! You want to like them and be liked. The People Likeability Factor" goes both ways, and it is the absolute most important criteria in your decision to accept a job offer. You want to be appreciated and inspired by your fellow employees and company leaders. Good people chemistry, cultural fit, and cooperative personalities are the key ingredients that make work

fun. Beware: you don't want to be the smartest person on the team. You need to be inspired by smart people around you. Being the sharpest arrow in the quiver will get old and boring. One of your primary reasons to join a new company should be to learn and expand your knowledge through your talented co-workers. This is accomplished by working with highly skilled and intelligent people who work well together and synergize off each other's individual strengths.

2. **CHALLENGE** – The actual work you will be doing in your new job must be challenging, or you will get very bored, very quickly, and find yourself climbing the walls. The "Role Challenge Factor" must be evident, or you will eventually be looking for a new job again in 6 months or less. To avoid choosing the wrong position and role in an organization, never settle for less responsibility than you can handle and always be thinking about the next level of increased management responsibilities. Does the new job opportunity include advancement as a reward for your above-average performance? If not, you risk the chance of not being challenged or inspired to deliver your best effort. You must be motivated to make a difference to achieve the company objectives and vision.

3. **BALANCE** – "Work and Life Balance Factor" is an important criterion because we do not live to work -- we work to live! A person who works 60-80 hours a week will not have much of life to enjoy the fruits of his/her labor. Keep in mind that each person's lifestyle changes as they progress during their career. Their children grow up, go away to school, move out and start lives and families of their own. Being a "Soccer Saturday" Dad or Mom is not a parent requirement anymore. At that point in your life, you have more freedom and flexibility to jump on a plane and travel out of town on business at a moment's notice. Your

time dedicated to the job is only relative to the current obligations to your family and friends.

4. **WORTH –** As in Salary. Will the company be able to pay you what you are worth in the form of annual salary (guaranteed cash compensation) plus incentives and stock options, etc., based on your "Worth Contribution Factor" to the new company? Keep in mind it's not all about money because "**Money is not a Motivator – it is a Stimulator!**" When a company decides they need you, they will have to induce (stimulate) you to accept their good faith offer of employment. Your compensation goal is always to remain whole and never settle for less. Do your homework to research management level pay scales to determine industry, function, and discipline competitiveness with similar companies.

The real secret to using these four criteria is to rank each of the Top 4 Criteria on a scale of 1-10 (10=ideal or best) to determine if your current job opportunity meets your essential needs and requirements. Anything criteria ranked less than seven is suspect and should not be ignored. Hint: These four criteria rankings should be used as your "**Negotiation Factors**" to make the right decision every time.

What is Your WHY?

"Your WHY is to inspire people to do what inspires them so that each of us can change and improve our world for the better." Mark James

Your **WHY** is your purpose, cause, or fundamental belief. It's the driving force behind all that you do. When you're at your best, your **HOWs** are your actions to bring your **WHY** to life. Your **WHATs** are the jobs you perform or the products/services you deliver. The WHY helps you in decision-making.

Making major decisions becomes more manageable when your **WHY** is positioned at the forefront of all you do. It helps you remember your values so that when it comes time to make decisions, you are doing what's best for you.

What is Your WHY in Your business? Quite simply, it's your purpose. It's what inspires you to take action. Your **WHY** inspires others to take action, spread your ideas, or buy your services and products.

What is Your WHY in Your Life? Your WHY is a statement of purpose that describes WHY you do the work you do and WHY you live your lifestyle. It is your calling. It is your conviction. It is your mission statement. It is a vision of your life and work.

What is an example of Your WHY?

"My WHY is to help people be more connected in their life, career, and business." Mark James

More specifically, to push me to be the best version of myself so that I know my mom is smiling down on me. To leave the world better than I found it and be remembered by the people whose lives I touched as a force for good in their lives.

Questions to determine Your WHY?

- Identify what you can do to improve other people's lives, businesses, and companies?
- Think back to the activities you did that made you forget about the passage of time?
- Recall what you liked to do when you were a kid. Try to capture the feelings you had that made you happy?
- Think about the biggest **WINS** in your career and how they made you feel?
- What led you to be who you are today and WHY?
- What were the events of your life that generated interest in your

current role, discipline, and function?

- What is your highest and best use, and WHY?
- What is your ideal company culture?
  - ✓ *I want to be part of a company that treats employees....?*
  - ✓ *I want to make a difference in people's lives by doing....?*
  - ✓ *I use my strengths/experiences to accomplish....?*

How to write a Personal "WHY" Statement

1. Begin by considering both who you are, who you want to become, and **WHY.**

2. Write down what is most important to you, what you want your legacy to be, and what you are most passionate about. If this is difficult, visualize what you hope your life will look like at the end of your career path and **WHY** you made a difference.

3. **WHY** not Dream Big? Take the time to articulate your Biggest Career Goals rather than writing down short-term plans.

4. Ask peers or mentors what they consider your biggest strengths to be, and consider **WHY** this makes you exceptional compared to others of similar expertise.

5. Consider what kind of mark you want to leave on the world and **WHY** your skills can help you achieve that.

6. Keep it short. If necessary, try a writing exercise in which you write down only five words that describe you and your purpose, then two, then one. Use these words as inspiration for your **WHY** statement.

7. Be true to yourself -- make sure your **WHY** statement accurately reflects your biggest passion and what you truly believe your long-term purpose to be.

"Learn how to interview effectively. Companies don't hire you for your reasons. They hire you for theirs." Mark James

Chapter 11

The Six Interview Mindsets

Keys to the Job Interview Mindset

Having a job interview mindset involves a conscious person's guide to better interviewing. In today's job market, the only job security is your ability to secure a job. What is relevant about The Interview Mindset is the fact that it works if you apply the methods and advice contained in this book.

Here is one important rule to note:

First and foremost, the interview is a conversation, NOT an interrogation! The interview is only an answer to part of the solution. We need to believe that conversation is an action step towards learning and making decisions. The only way to have meaningful conversations and creative dialogue is to ask really good questions. The critical task is to find the right questions, ones that are open-ended enough to engage anyone in a productive conversation.

There are a lot of lessons you've learned that handle a lot of potential interview bombshells that come your way, like "What's your greatest lesson?" or "What's your biggest weakness?" or "What's the most embarrassing aspect of your career?" If you don't answer those questions right, it's the kiss of death. If you come off as "I've never made mistakes" or "I don't have any weaknesses," that's impossible. If your ego enters the room before you physically walk through the door, you're going to get rejected right away. It's the quickest way to be rejected when the ego flies. The question, in many cases, is the answer. There's no sound bite.

Instead, it's important to get the question right. Most of us are busy answering the wrong questions. Try answering these questions instead: What are your commitments? What is worth doing? What do you love doing? Why would you hire you? What do you do best? Are you a buyer or seller? Are you a leader or a follower? How do you make a difference? What matters most? Where is the pain? What do you need to do to be successful? What didn't the last person do that you (Mr. Hiring Manager Name?) really needed them to accomplish?

What Matters Most

In every employment interview, there is always one party that likes the other party more than the other. The hiring process is like a courtship that can begin slowly and end quickly. It can also start fast and develop into a long-term relationship. Remember this: there are coincidences when it comes to interviews. Of course, you would never get an interview if there was no interest from both parties. There must be a need and a want for the process to begin. The first interview is always an interesting setup...almost like a blind date.

Do you really know your career goals? I am a firm believer that if you don't' know what you want -- that's what you will probably get – Nothing! What makes you happy? If you can create the ideal job for yourself, what would it look like? How much autonomy, responsibility, and accountability will you have? Are you a people person who wants to make a difference in other peoples' careers? Are you likable?

Interview Mindset Defined

In every interview, your personal leadership qualities will be under scrutiny to a much greater extent than in previous recruitment processes. To shine, your attitude and mindset will be just as important as your technical and leadership competencies.

If you don't think you can do the job, don't go to the interview. If you think you can do the job, then your behaviors must demonstrate that you do. There is no middle ground.

The logic is straightforward. If you don't demonstrate confidence in your ability to make a difference in a company, why should the "Decision Makers" (DM) have confidence in you? After all, they are making what will probably be their single most important decision - choosing the right person for the job. It's not unreasonable to expect that they might be worried about making the wrong decision and be a little risk-averse as a consequence.

As a short-listed or final candidate, you start with important psychological advantages. First, congratulations, you are a short-listed candidate. You have been narrowed down to a large number of candidates, and your skills and competencies must have connected with the D.M. on some level. You are already ahead of the game and have earned leverage.

Second, the D.M. desperately wants you to succeed at the interview. They start each interview wanting the candidate in front of them to be the solution to the problem of finding a new employee. No executive committee or selection panel starts out with the aim of not making an appointment. So, your job as a candidate is to make sure the company has no reason not to appoint you to the position. In short, the decision-makers have got to believe that you are their next employee to be hired. And this is where the right mindset is key.

There is so much more than just having a mindset when you're in an interview. You have to have a plan. Please refer to the 22 interview questions with answer strategies listed further in this chapter. You will need to develop your accomplishment stories and examples. Get ready BEFORE you walk through the door for your interview at the company.

Here are The Six Interview Mindsets

Mindset #1 - The Doctor/Patient Mindset. When I talk about a mindset, it's sort of like they pretend that you play the doctor and the hiring manager is the patient. When you are sick and visit the doctor, he or she asks questions to determine your condition, so they can help. It's the exact same process during the interview. That's the doctor/patient mindset.

Mindset #2 - The Consulting Mindset. Act as a consultant. You're looking for problems that require solutions. What would you do differently in an interview if you had the mindset that you were acting as a consultant? You're trying to understand what the issues are, what the problems are because that's what a consultant has to do. They have to understand how they're going to be able to help them. By the way, in that doctor/patient mindset, as you're determining whether or not they have problems, your question to them, as an interviewer, *is "What are the top five or six critical deliverables that the person that gets this job needs to do in the next six to twelve months?"*

It's the absolute number one question to ask right out of the box when you get a chance. Then you're saying that this person needs to do that, needs to do this. You're not nominating yourself too soon because you don't know whether or not you want to do this job yet.

What if they give you menial types of responsibilities and goals that you used to do 10-15 years ago? Then that's going to be a challenging problem. You're not going to feel challenged on the job. Your job is to find out what those deliverables are, and if you're really good and you're good to go with your examples and stories, you can pull one of those examples out that matches up with one of the things that they bring up as one of the greatest deliverables or issues that they need to have this person solve in the next 6-12 months.

Mindset #3 - Pretend it's the First Day on the Job. You're thinking to yourself, "I've got this job. What am I going to do? How am I going to act?" You'll be confident, enthusiastic, and excited. You want to be in the moment, and you're going to go in there and try to figure out what the boss needs to be done. What's keeping him up at night? What are the big objectives for the day or the week or the month that the boss needs to have completed? You're enthusiastic. Your mindset is different when you think of it going into an interview.

Mindset #4 - Be a Buyer - Not a Seller. I love this mindset. You don't know if you want this job yet. Don't sell too soon. Don't brag too soon. Don't start crowing about your great examples and stories BEFORE you know what the Hiring Manager (HM) and company needs?

That's a big Sales 101 mistake. Where do you start doing a feature and benefits presentation before you even ask the customer what is needed?

You have to know that before you start delivering a solution or a remedy or answer to their problem. Buyer versus a seller. When you're a buyer, you're asking good, compelling questions like "Why would somebody want to work here?" You don't know yet. You're not nominating yourself too soon. You're asking, "What does a person need to do to be successful?" Not "What do I need to do to be successful should you bring me on board?"

Don't nominate yourself too soon. Remember — be a **Human Switzerland and Stay Neutral.** There will be a time when you need to convert over and be totally committed and ready to take on this challenge, but you have to determine whether they really can keep you motivated, and is this going to be challenging? That's very important.

Mindset #5 - Pretend You Won the Lotto. The final mindset is kind of a fun one where you drive home, and you pick up the groceries, and you buy a lotto ticket, and you use that lotto ticket as a prop to pretend that you've won the lotto. $500,000,000, and you know you're going into an interview the first thing tomorrow with the C.E.O. and the chairman of the board. You pick up the paper in the morning, and you realize that all your numbers match up and you've won millions of dollars. Do you still go on the interview, or do you not?

What would your mindset be if you pretended that you'd won the lotto and went on the interview? How would you act differently? What would you say? What would you do? You know there's nothing they can say to ruin your day because you've just won $500,000,000. You could actually buy the company if you were so inclined.

It's an interesting mindset because now you are more relaxed. You're more comfortable. You're going to be more likable. You might even have fun because you're learning about an opportunity, and what's going on in their company might be very exciting to you, but you might also think this isn't the right fit. Those are the five mindsets.

In other words, saying that you should answer a question X, Y, Z is not nearly as powerful as showing them, "Well, if you answer it wrong like this, this is what happens." Like selling yourself too soon. Some people that you may know might have started selling themselves right from the beginning and then realized that they didn't want the job at all, under any circumstances. The key is to not allow the H.M. to think you need the job more than the company needs you. Don't be aloof or act like you are interested...just keep in mind you have choices, too!

What happens is they may believe that you are desperate, especially if you're out of work. If you need them more than they need you, they may think, "Well, jeez, we've got John in our back pocket. We know he really wants to work here. Bring in the next candidate, so we can compare and contrast that person with John." But if you give them the impression that you're not 100% on board, you're still determining, and then it's a two-way street. You've got to look at them as much as they're looking at you because these are critical decisions. These are business decisions, and you cannot afford to join the company for the wrong reasons.

In fact, there are statistics that show 50% of people that take the first job offer that comes their way, when they're out of work, 50% of the time they're looking for a new job in six months because they jumped too soon. They ignored the red flags and the yellow flags because they just wanted to get back in the ranks and get on the payroll. They settled for less, and now they're regretting it, and it's ten times worse now. Maybe more.

Mindset #6 – Honesty + Ethics + Integrity. Along with projecting Confidence and Enthusiasm during the job interview, you must address your reputation of possessing **Honesty, Ethics, and Integrity**, which can never be in short supply in business.

A person's character often determines how successful they are in any career. Having a solid work ethic, remaining honest, and demanding self-integrity will be noticed on the job. Employers typically seek and promote workers that encompass these qualities. These three extraordinary characteristics must be the hallmark of your job interview narrative. When asked what your career strengths, skills, or competencies are – ALWAYS include Honesty, Ethics, and Integrity.

Honesty
Regardless of the job, honest behavior is crucial. Modifying a time card, filling out an expense report, allowing someone else to take the blame for your mistakes, or exaggerating circumstances on the job are all forms of dishonesty. Once an employer catches an employee or applicant in a lie, that employee may be fired or summarily dismissed from the hiring process. If the employee is not fired, that seed of doubt will be planted in the employer's mind. This may cause an employer to question the worker's honesty from then on.

Ethics

In general, ethics are directly linked to moral principles. Ethics is the ability to tell the difference between right and wrong. Although an individual may know something is wrong, a good work ethic keeps him from taking that wrongful action. Work ethic is applying this principle on the job. When an employee exhibits a strong work ethic, they become a vital asset.

Integrity

Integrity can be described as the strength of someone's honesty and ethical standing. A person with solid integrity is less likely to be influenced by lesser moral values. Employers want to know that a worker will remain honest regardless of a co-worker's actions. Integrity reflects good moral character.

Getting Ready for The Interview

From the first moment you set foot over the threshold of the company doors to begin an interview and selection process, your outlook and behaviors must be those of a prospective employee – not an applicant. At every stage of the selection process – during formal and informal moments – the decision-makers must see you as their next employee. The key is to treat everyone you meet like they are a major customer or client you could lose. Kindness matters.

This doesn't mean that you won't have development needs or gaps in your knowledge to fill – but it does mean that you demonstrate the outlook and behavior of someone who is already at the required leadership and management level and can communicate what it is for the employer, should they desire to hire you. Learn and anticipate about the company's hiring process they use to know they have the right candidate BEFORE you sit down with the interviewer. It is a fair question to ask in advance: What is your hiring process? # of interviews? etc.

The Exit Statement

The other question that everybody gets stuck on is, **"Why did you leave your last job?"** Or "Why are you looking to make a job change now at this time in your career?" If you don't have an air-tight answer, you're definitely going to have problems. If it's not credible, believable, or understandable, then they could have that tinge of doubt throughout the whole interview because you never answered it properly. You never gave them a real reason to say, "Hey, I get that. That makes a lot of sense."

The exit statement is why you are leaving or why you are looking for a new job. If you don't answer that right, they may never let you know that they don't believe you, or it doesn't make sense, or they're not sold on your answer. The next thing is they're passing on you, and you don't even know why. That's a mistake that people make a lot. Probably the biggest mistake in an interview is not being ready for the exit statement.

These are the little things that they couldn't do on their own and wouldn't know unless there was somebody with them as they were role-playing and doing a mock interview. Basically, the tough questions are, "Why did you leave your last job?" Or, "Why are you looking for a new job?" And the answer needs to be a very well-crafted exit statement.

The Exit Statement is known as the **Reason for Leaving or Looking.** And recruiters typically refer to that as **R.F.L.** It can be a catchall, and they want to know what the motivation is for making a job change or what happened in their last assignment or job.

Recruiters always want to know the reason for leaving or looking. What's the motivation behind the job search? Interviewers are going to ask that question; they want to see, they want to look in their eyes, and that answer can sink or swim any candidate. You need to be honest when answering these questions.

If you don't answer it convincingly, with credibility, believability, and it's understood, meaning if it's confusing or they dance around the answer, or they don't get to the real reason, well, now there's doubt. When doubt creeps into the R.F.L., you've got a problem. The interview may not go very well. You may never recover if you don't handle the R.F.L. You've got to cover it really well.

What I have created here is more of a visual, is a formatted approach to the R.F.L. The reason for leaving, and its visual. It's an Oreo cookie. Oreo cookies, as we know, have three parts. You've got the top chocolate part of the cookie, the white stuff in the middle, and the bottom part of the cookie. And this is how you format and structure the R.F.L.

The "OREO Cookie" R.F.L. Statement Format

The Top Part of the Cookie has to be a positive statement. It starts out like, "In my last assignment with A.B.C. Company, I really enjoyed working with that company over a period of x years. I've made some incredible accomplishments and made some incredibly great professional friendships.

The White Stuff in the Middle. "However, over the last year, we lost two of our biggest clients, the company was put up for sale, they reorganized, the new hiring C.E.O. came in with his own team. It totally affected the impact of my role within the company, and my position was eliminated." That's the stuff in the middle.

The Bottom Part of the Cookie is another positive statement. And essentially, you say, "However, this has given me a fantastic opportunity to explore new companies such as yours, Mr. Hiring Authority at A.B.C. company, where my background, expertise, and wisdom will have mutual benefits with your needs and the company's vision, growth, and plan for the future." Something that is going to resonate with them. They need to really capture the whole gist of the statement.

This needs to be rehearsed; it needs to be scripted out, first of all, then rehearsed, and they need to be able to replay it in an unrehearsed way. This is not that difficult, as long as you practice. But when it sounds like a script, and you're robotic in the way that you're reciting something, it doesn't come off as authentic and genuine as it should.

If you're comfortable reciting your own answer, the OREO Cookie formatted R.F.L., then they'll be comfortable. If you sound uncertain, if you sound like you're winging it, if you sound like you're making it up as you go along, it's not going to work. And you need to be really, really good at delivering the R.F.L., or you'll never get into the important part of the interview, which is, "What have you done in your last job or assignment? More importantly, HOW did you do it?" Whatever that significant example is that you made an impact within the company.

The Positioning Statement *(The 2-minute Elevator Pitch)*

Let's look at this common interview question: **Tell me about yourself?** Sounds simple, right? This is one of those "break the ice" kinds of statements that open it up for a long discussion about who you are and what you represent, what makes you tick. There's a right way and a wrong way to answer that question. The wrong way is where they just go ahead and recite their resume after they graduate from school all the way to their current job. It's boring. No one wants to hear your whole career path story in one two-minute answer because it's impossible to do.

Important Tip: NEVER recite your resume to anyone <u>EVER</u>!

I always say that if you don't know what they are looking for, based on the question, you can reply, "Where would you like me to start?" Let them be more specific. The reason they say, "Tell me about yourself, John," is because there are a lot of questions that can't be asked legally. I call it the "vomit question" because they're getting people to vomit. They talk too much. They share too much. Irrelevant things. It starts the interview off in a very awkward moment. The answer to the question is your positioning statement. It's the two-minute elevator pitch that everybody talks about. If you're not really good and it's not rehearsed, and you don't really have a good elevator pitch, well, you better have one.

Develop your P.L.A.N.

Having a job interview **P.L.A.N.** is essential. You have to know what your answers will be. Prepare to discuss your **PASSIONS, LESSONS ACCOMPLISHMENTS, and NEEDS.** Once you are comfortable addressing these four areas – you will be on your way to eliminating the competition.

The Bookend Answer Approach

This approach is a great way for you to frame your answer. When somebody says, "Why should we hire you for this job?" you say, "I believe you should hire me for this job because…" That's the front side of the bookend, and then you deliver your content answer in the middle. Reflect on your top eight competencies that you can frame sentences around, paying particular attention to the top three to five (out of 8) key attributes or characteristics that demonstrate your qualifications, strengths, abilities, and competencies. And when you finish that answer, you bookend it by saying, "That's why I believe you should hire me for this job."

The beautiful thing is that they hear it three times. They say it once, they hear you say it one time at the beginning of the bookend, and then they hear it again at the end of your answer. And it's almost like a positive reinforcement type of thing. And it does work. You don't want to do it with a question like, "What's your greatest weakness?" "Oh, my greatest weakness is..." and then you say something, and then you say, "That's my greatest weakness." You don't want to emphasize the greatest weakness with the bookend approach.

This system has worked for me several times. The bookending is a good way to start, and then you don't just drop off a cliff trying to end your answer; you come to the end of it, and then you very confidently say, "That's why I believe you should hire me for this job."

The "tell me about yourself" question is an open-ended question that is designed to get people to go off on tangents and talk about their life, their family, their upbringing, their schooling, their current relatable activity, and their most recent job. The problem is that the "tell me about yourself" is known as the vomit question because people don't know where to start. They don't know what to say sometimes. They're not prepared, and they just start talking about themselves, and they volunteer stuff that is irrelevant to the conversation.

The proper answer is a positioning statement, which is known as what? The two-minute elevator pitch. It's essentially, who are you? What's your highest and best use, and what are your greatest deliverables that you believe are invaluable to a company? It's a description of what you were meant to do in your career, what you enjoy doing, what you delivered, and how you get things done. Your method, your steps, your processes, and make it personal. This is the first, maybe the second, question out of the box for most interviews, especially a phone screen over the phone. And companies want to get you talking.

If you start reciting your resume, that's the kiss of death; it's really not going to get you any more points by reciting a resume. In fact, you should never recite the resume unless the interviewer actually asks you to. "Tell me about your first job out of college, and bring me up to the current time as we speak in your most recent job." If they say that, then you do it in two minutes or less.

The answer to the positioning statement is essentially the most relevant info that is probably within the last three to five years. Who you are, what you've become, what you represent, how you make a difference — your passion for what you do? The satisfaction and reward of performing incredible accomplishments and achievements in your current or former role with the company you work for or previously worked for.

This could be done in two minutes or less without a lot of rambling. As long as it's a scripted statement, and you memorize it and practice so it sounds unrehearsed. And there could be varying lengths. That could be a 30-second, a one-minute, a one-minute-thirty seconds; it's up to them to determine how much information they want to share that gets the interviewer comfortable with the answer.

There is another strategy that when someone says tell me about yourself, you can say, "Where would you like me to start?" Let them tell you. Throw it back to them. It's okay to ask a question to a question. Our mothers said don't ask a question to the question, just answer the question. But it's okay to do that.

In an interview, if you need more info, if it's not clear, ask, "Can you rephrase the question? I'm not quite sure I understand what you're asking." But in this case, then tell me about yourself is such an open-ended question that it's fair to say, "Where would you like me to start?"

Remember – Never EVER recite your resume! It's boring and it will put the interviewer to sleep.

Mock Interviews

To exercise your mind, it is ideal to hold a series of mock interviews. You should do a mock interview with somebody who has done this before. Not just your spouse or brother or your sister but somebody who is a neutral contracted third party. A professional career coach is a good choice. They are there to help as a trusted advisor who will be honest and direct about how you did. They're not going to pull any punches when they need to really let you know, "You can't say that," or "You know what? You're coming off a little too egotistical," or something like that. Those are the things that people don't do.

The interview practice is extremely critical. No actor would go on stage without rehearsing a dozen times. It's the most important meeting of your life. You shouldn't be winging it. Then we've got the actual interview itself, but we also have a section on networking to get you to the interview.

When I'm speaking or I am facilitating my networking meetings, I ask for a show of hands, *"How many people have gone through a professional mock interview training session?"* Maybe 3 out of 30 people raise their hand. I say, "Folks, you got to think about this. If your son or daughter has a big final exam at school tomorrow morning, are you going to say go ahead and kick a soccer ball or shoot some baskets or are you going to have them go upstairs and suggest they really get ready for the exam?"

It's the same thing with you. It's probably even more important because you have to get that job offer to make ends meet with your family. Are you going to go into the interview with the C.E.O. or the owner of the business and wing it? Or are you going to go to the bar or go to the bowling alley tonight? What are you going to do? You're going to get ready for that interview. Why not do a mock interview and be ultimately prepared? The ultimate preparation for a job interview is to be ready to eliminate the competition. Not just separate yourself but eliminate the other people who are competing for the same job. If you're not that well prepared, then someone else is going to get the offer. Pretty simple.

You eliminate the competition by performing really well during your mock interview, and then this translates to doing well in the main interview. It's the power of visualization and manifestation.

When you do a mock interview, you see how well you are doing in a practice session in light of the fact that you are going to make mistakes. There are no judgment calls, but when you do fumble through an answer, you have to go back and get critiqued. You fix and you update and you make it perfect. You have to be ready for the tough ones that come your way.

22 Tough Interview Questions with Answer Strategies

Here are some sample questions. Try them out and get a professional to tell you how well you did!

1. Can you tell me about yourself?

Just talk for two minutes. Be logical. Start with college or your first job...OR ask, "Where would you like me to start?" The interviewer is looking for communication skills and linear thinking, so bear in mind that seemingly innocuous question such as "Tell me about yourself" is actually, "Why are you the ideal candidate for this position?" The best answers are honest, confident, and concise. Also, score a point or two by describing your major attribute. Hint: Use your Positioning Statement.

2. Why are you leaving your current position/last job?

This is a very critical question. Don't "bad mouth" your previous employer. Don't sound "too opportunistic." Best to relate major industry problems, a buy-out, shutdown, re-org, or downsizing. Also good is to state that after long personal consideration, a chance to make a contribution is very low due to company changes. **Hint: Use your Exit Statement.**

3. What do you consider your most significant accomplishment?
This can get you the job. Prepare extensively. Score points. Tell a two-minute story, with details, and discuss personal involvement. Make the accomplishment worth achieving. Discuss hard work, long hours, pressure, and important company issues at stake. Most importantly, tell them "HOW" you did it. You must create a value perception before the meeting has ended!

4. Why do you believe you are qualified for this position?
Pick two or three main factors about you and your job that are most relevant. Discuss for two minutes with specific details. Select a technical skill, a specific management skill (organizing, staffing, planning, leadership), and a personal success attribute to mention.

5. Have you ever accomplished something you didn't think you could?
The interviewer is trying to determine your goal orientation, work ethic, personal commitment, and integrity. Provide a good example where you overcame numerous difficulties to succeed. Prove you're not a quitter and "that you'll get going when the going gets tough."

6. What do you like/dislike most about your current/previous position?
The interviewer is trying to determine compatibility with the open position. If you have an interest in the position, be careful. Stating that you dislike overtime or getting into details or that you like "management" can cost you the position. There is nothing wrong with liking challenges, pressure situations, opportunities to grow, or disliking bureaucracy and frustrating situations.

7. How do you handle pressure situations? Do you like or dislike these situations?

High achievers tend to perform well in high-pressure situations. Conversely, the question also could imply that the position is pressure-packed and out of control. There is nothing wrong with this as long as you know what you're getting into. If you do perform well under stress, provide a good example with details giving an overview of the stress situation. Let the interviewer "feel" the stress by your description of it. Use a "Philosophy + Real Life Example" answer approach.

8. Give me an example of where you have demonstrated initiative?

The sign of a good employee is the ability to take the initiative. A proactive, results-oriented person doesn't have to be told what to do.

This is one of the major success attributes. To convince the interviewer you possess this trait, you must give a series of short examples describing your self-motivation. Try to discuss at least one example in-depth. The extra effort, strong work ethic, and creative side of you must be demonstrated.

9. What's the worst or most embarrassing aspect of your business career?

How would you have done things differently now with 20/20 hindsight? This is a general question to learn how introspective you are and to see if you can learn from your mistakes. If you can, it indicates an open, more flexible personality. Don't be afraid to talk about your failures, particularly if you learned from them. This is a critical aspect of high-potential individuals.

10. How have you grown or changed over the past few years?

This requires thought. Maturation, increased technical skills, or increased self-confidence are important aspects of human development. To discuss this effectively is indicative of a well-balanced, intelligent individual. Overcoming personal obstacles or recognizing manageable weaknesses can brand you as an approachable and desirable employee.

11. Why would you hire you? (What are your most significant strengths?)

Be prepared. Know your Top 8 Competencies. (Your career acronym) Create a passionate sentence for every strength. Select those attributes that are most compatible with the job opening. Most people say "management" or "good interpersonal skills" in answer to this. Don't, unless you can describe the specific characteristics of management (planning, organizing, results, hiring, staffing, recruiting, etc.) and/or how your relationship skills have proven critical to your success. Use a "Bookend Answer" approach.

12. What do you consider your most significant weaknesses?

Don't reveal deep character flaws. Rather, discuss tolerable faults that you are working towards improving. Show by specific examples how this has changed over time. Better still, show how a weakness can be turned into a strength. For example, how a concentration on the details results in higher quality work even though it requires much overtime.

13. Deadlines, frustrations, difficult people, and silly rules can make a job difficult. How do you handle these types of situations?

Most companies, unfortunately, face these types of problems daily. If you can't deal with petty frustrations, you'll be seen as a problem. You certainly can state your displeasure at the petty side of these issues, but how you overcome them is more important. Diplomacy, perseverance, and common sense can often prevail even in difficult circumstances. This is part of corporate America, and you must be able to deal with it on a regular basis.

14. One of the biggest problems is _____. Can you describe your most comparable accomplishment? How would you implement this task or project?

Think on your feet. Ask questions to get details. Break it into sub-parts. Highly likely you have some experience with the sub-sections. Answer these, and summarize the total. State how you would go about solving the problem. Be specific. Show your organizational and analytical skills.

15. Give me an example of when you executed a project flawlessly?

The ability to get the job done, regardless of any obstacles that come up along the way, is a key trait of top performers. Failure to execute is one of the top reasons people fail. Be ready to describe another great story or example that demonstrates your competencies.

16. Tell me about your biggest team-directed accomplishment in a difficult time or situation?

Top performers get the job done by utilizing the talents of others. No one can do it all. Top performers know this, and leading a team is something they are good at. Relating a strong example of your leadership skills is a strong predictor of future performance.

17. How do you compare your technical skills to your management skills?

Many people tend to minimize their technical skills, either because they don't have any or they don't like getting into detail. Most successful managers possess good technical skills and get into enough detail to make sure they understand the information being presented by their group. Try for a good balance here if you want to be seriously considered for the position.

18. How has your technical ability been important in accomplishing results?

Clearly, the interviewer believes he needs a strong level of technical competence and resourcefulness. Most strong managers have good technical backgrounds, even if they have gotten away from the detail. Describe specific examples of your technical wherewithal, but don't be afraid to say you are not current. Also, you could give an example of how you resolved a technical issue by "accelerated research."

19. How would you handle a situation with tight deadlines, low employee morale, and inadequate resources?

If you pull this off effectively, it indicates you have strong management skills. Be creative. An example would be great. Relate your toughest management task, even if it doesn't meet all the criteria. Most situations don't. Organizational skills, interpersonal skills, and handling pressure are key elements of effective management. Good managers should be able to address each issue, even if they were not concurrent. Deftly handling the question is pretty indicative of your skills, too.

20. Are you satisfied with your career to date? What would you change if you could?

Be honest. The interviewer wants to know if they can keep you happy. It's important to know if you're willing to make some sacrifices to get your career on the right track. The degree of motivation is an important selection criterion.

21. What are your career goals? Where do you see yourself five years from now?

Most importantly, be realistic! Blue sky stuff brands you as immature. One or two management jumps in 3-5 years is a reasonable goal. If your track indicates you're in line for senior management in 10 years, it's okay to mention. However, if you've had a rocky road, better to be introspective. Hint: Use your Professional Objective Statement.

22. Why should we hire you for this position? What kind of contribution would you make?

This is a good chance to summarize. By now, you know the key problems. Re-state and show how you would address it. Relate to specific attributes and to specific accomplishments. Qualify responses with the need to gather information. Don't be cocky. Demonstrate a thoughtful, organized, strong effort kind of attitude.

Be Prepared – Non-Verbal Communication

Now that you are armed with some likely questions, do a two and a half to three-hour mock interview and go through every one of these questions. For my clients, I go over this with them. Together we break down and tweak their answer after each question. If they nailed it and they did a really good job, then we say don't change a thing; that's perfect. Now they know. Peace of mind that they've got that answer without any problem.

But if they need to work on it and they need to get their frame of mind, and they want to get used to saying whatever they are going to say, we can play it back and do it again and see how well they do the second time around. The goal is to correct any evident issues and things they are not comfortable saying or it comes off as negative. I'm also looking at their eyes, the tone of their voice, their body language, facial expressions, etc. Neurolinguistics Programming (N.L.P.), which is the study of non-verbal communication, is really important.

On the other hand, a lot of people in hiring, like human resources, are aware of N.L.P., and some of them are practitioners and certified, so they can tell when somebody's making it up or telling the truth. It's in the eyes and in the tone of their voice. Those things are reviewed, and I bring them up in case they're not really giving me good eye contact and they're tentative in the tone of their voice. If they end on a high note, I get a little concerned that they're not really comfortable giving the answer. It's almost as if they're seeking approval like, "Is that the right answer, Mr. Hiring Authority?" Whereas, if they end on a down note, it is a lot more authoritative. It's a lot more credible, believable, and understandable.

Zoom Job Interview Tips

When you are interviewing virtually, there are some things you should do—and things you shouldn't—if you want to make the best impression. Companies are shifting from in-person to remote interviews, so it's essential to interview by video call. In a recent survey of talent leaders and recruiters, 80% of respondents said their hiring process is entirely remote. In comparison, 39% have increased their video conferencing software, like Zoom, for the interview process.

That's good news if you are looking for work because you can interview for jobs from the comfort of home. However, virtual interviewing comes with its own set of challenges, especially if you're not used to meeting remotely. It's all too easy to get flustered by the technology and forget to mind the details that make the difference between a so-so interview and one that clinches a job offer.

Increase your chances of making a good impression and getting the job. There are inevitable mistakes you should avoid before and during Zoom interviews:

1. Arrive Early to the Online Interview
When it comes to job interviews, if you're not early, you're late. It's never okay to be late for a tee time or doctor's appointment. It's even more important for Zoom interviews. Jump on the call a few minutes early, and you won't have to worry about last-minute technical difficulties derailing your effort. There's nothing worse than starting a job interview stressed out and distracted. Always confirm your interview details before the day of your meeting to make sure you're on time and prepared.

2. Practice With the Technology Beforehand
Speaking of technical difficulties, you can avoid many of them by making sure you're comfortable with the software ahead of time. Be sure to download Zoom and get in at least one practice interview before the actual event. You'll feel more at ease during the conversation and more resilient if other technical issues arise.

3. Gather Your Documents and Materials

Once you're seated in front of your computer, you should be able to reach everything you need to carry out a successful interview. Ensure you have all your interview materials, i.e., your resume, references, portfolio, etc., and that you're comfortable and ready to speak.

Although you shouldn't eat or drink during the conversation, you should have a glass of water ready in an emergency. (Interview nerves can cause dry mouth, so it's better to take a sip of water than to cough your way through the meeting.)

4. Dress to Impress

An ounce of image is worth a pound of performance. If you are accustomed to being at home in sweats or pajamas for an extended period, it might be hard to remember what professional attire is appropriate. Business attire or casual attire is usually the best bet for job interviews. A suit, sportscoat, button-down, or nice sweater are safe bets. Try to peg your outfit to the company's culture as you understand it, but do dress up a bit, even if employees keep it super-casual.

Remember that whatever you choose should show well on camera and be professional. Avoid stripes, extremely bright colors, or wearing the same shade as your background.

Even if the interviewer can't see the lower half of your body, it's a good idea to wear appropriate attire. You'll conduct yourself more professionally and avoid showing off your pajama pants if you need to stand up for some reason.

5. Present a Professional Background with Good Lighting

Zoom allows you to choose a default background image or upload your professional headshot photo. Make sure the lighting in the room is adequate. Buy an inexpensive light ring with a tri-pod to plug into an open USB port in your computer or laptop. By all means, if you don't use a virtual background, clean up and organize your room to present a professional experience. Why? Research shows that your work environment affects your mental health and decision-making ability. In short, a quiet workspace promotes peace of mind.

6. Avoid Distracting Habits

Perhaps the worst Zoom interview mistake you can make is to indicate that you're not interested in what the interviewer is saying through your behavior and mannerisms. Unfortunately, this is easier to do than you might think.

Little gestures can make a significant impact. Fidgeting with your hair or your clothes, checking your phone (yes, even off-screen), or staring at yourself instead of connecting with the interviewer—all these can make it seem like you're disconnected or distracted.

7. Carry on a Real Conversation

Some job interviews can feel like interrogations, even face to face. Video technology can exacerbate this problem by shrinking your visual field down to two screens and ratcheting up the tension with the threat of technical difficulties.

To overcome these issues, remind yourself that a good job interview is a conversation—no more and no less. You and the interviewer are not on opposing sides but on the same team, working toward a common goal.

Focus on listening instead of waiting for your chance to speak. You'll demonstrate valuable soft skills (EQ), communicate better, and learn more about the job. Best of all, you'll make a more favorable impression on the hiring manager, which is essential to helping you land the job.

8. Make the Best Impression

Practice makes perfect: This may not always be the case, but if you take the time to ensure you prepare and your technology is working correctly, the interview will be much less stressful.

Get set ahead of time: Don't wait until the last minute to set up your interview space, clear away the clutter, and get your interview clothes ready.

Please pay attention: It can be hard when you're interviewing remotely, so remember to listen carefully to the questions and focus on your interviewer.

Chapter 12

The Job Offer Checklist

Congratulations! After a long and arduous job search, you've got yourself a job offer. But how do you know if it's a good one? Deciding to accept a job can be a big decision, and evaluating a job offer isn't easy. It's crucial to understand how to evaluate a job offer before deciding whether you can negotiate for something better.

As the saying goes, ***"Don't love something that does not love you back."***

Evaluating a job offer is not simple and should be done carefully. Statistically, your leverage to tailor your job description, increase your salary, and improve your benefits is most vital at the job offer stage than at any point. Now is the ultimate time to negotiate and close all loose ends and get the offer the way you want it. Assess the offer based on your needs. Hopefully, you have researched whether the offer is competitive and fair based on your city and state, cost of living, commute distance, etc.

Besides the headliner metrics like salary, job title, and responsibilities, you should also consider aspects contributing to your overall happiness and job satisfaction. There is no perfect job offer – but with an honest assessment and negotiating the exemplary aspects, you can tweak any job offer to better suit your needs.

In this chapter, I will review the main aspects that you should be evaluating when assessing any job offer and provide worksheets to evaluate job offers.

How to Assess a Job Offer

1. Salary plus bonus/incentives

Consider all compensation. Even when you think the offered salary is adequate, is the market rate considering your qualifications? Compensation packages these days are often multi-faceted – base salary, bonus/incentive packages, share award schemes, and pensions all contribute to the monetary aspect of any job offer.

What is the market rate? Continually benchmark the compensation of a job offer to know where you stand. Databases like Glassdoor, Salary.com, and Payscale.com are good starting points to find more salary data. Don't just check one website – check them and compare your research notes.

Negotiation: If you plan to negotiate on salary, have a strong reason (or set of causes) why you should be offered a higher package. It would help if you also had a backup plan – assess other aspects of the job, such as an early salary review based on your above-average performance. You can also ask for a percentage (50%) of your first year's bonus to be guaranteed during your new job assimilation ramp-up period.

2. Opportunities for growth

Would you prefer to be leading a big team, a few people, or none at all? There are several aspects to this, and you must assess them honestly:

- ✓ **Training and Development:** Do you deserve more responsibility based on your previous role?
- ✓ **Autonomy:** Do you want opportunities for promotion to added management responsibilities and more freedom and independence to make decisions?
- ✓ **Individual Contributor:** Do you naturally enjoy managing and interacting with people, or do you prefer a role as an individual contributor?

- ✓ **Travel requirements.** What degree of traveling would the job require, and does that fit into your current life and family obligations? Will this allow you to have a 50/50 work-life balance?
- ✓ **Team interaction.** Depending on your personality, do you prefer to work in large teams, smaller teams, or with as few people as possible?
- ✓ **Client-facing time:** Do you want to be client-facing to develop your relationship management skills and improve your professional network, or would you rather free up valuable time to focus on developing your core professional skills?

3. Leadership Development

Skill development. While you'll almost always learn something new in any role, you should consider whether the development opportunities offered are in sync with your long-term plans. For example, suppose you have extensive experience and skills in research and want to spend more time developing your presentation and communication skills. In that case, you might prefer a role with more opportunities to face internal or external clients.

Long-term goals. Is the job setting you up in the right direction in your long-term career path? If the roles you're considering aren't quite yet in your ideal industry, prioritize the ones that are at least another step in the right direction. If you're looking to build management skills, you might choose a role with team members reporting to you, even if the other positions offer better perks or better pay.

4. Cultural fit

Will I be happy here? You'll also need to judge whether you'd enjoy working there. It's challenging to know for sure without actually spending proper time there. Reach out to your contacts and LinkedIn network to get a better idea. Ask them about their firm's opinion, how long people tend to stay, or what happened to the last person who did the job. Glassdoor also provides pretty comprehensive employee reviews of their workplace culture for larger companies.

5. Quality of life

Vacation and work flexibility. Vacation time and the ability to work flexible hours are increasingly valuable perks. If flexible work hours are high up on your priority list and not explicitly given in your work contract, raising this in the negotiation stage is a good idea. **Working remotely and Telecommuting perks.** Consider negotiating working remotely from home 2 or 3 days each week to avoid long time-wasting commutes. Research bicycle paths, train ticket perks, company cars, or any other travel-related perk and how it would fit into your work commuting plan.

Your Manager and Co-Workers

One of the most critical "happiness and unhappiness factors" at work is related to working with your boss and co-workers. Here's something they'll probably never teach you in business school. The most significant decisions you make in your job – more prominent than the rest – are the people you report to and work arm-to-arm. The primary reason people quit their job is because of personality conflict, unsatisfying management relationships, and poor communication.

Job Offer Comparison Checklist

When considering job opportunities, it's essential to consider all elements of the offer and compensation package, both the tangible factors such as salary and benefits and the intangibles like location, work environment, and growth potential. You can use this checklist to evaluate and compare any job offers you might receive:

- Before considering definite opportunities, think about your specific circumstances and rank the listed elements in order of importance to you – **Section II, III Importance Ranking**

- Once you have received an offer(s), fill in the company and position for each offer you are considering - **Section I**
- Fill in as much information as possible based on the offer package(s) you have received. Under the quantitative side, make sure to consider what you would pay for the different elements as well as what the company would pay – **Section II, III**
- List the pros and cons of each position you are considering – **Section IV**
- Don't forget to listen to your instincts. If you don't feel that the opportunity is right for you, it probably isn't.

Section I
Offer #1 Company: **Job Title:**
Offer #2 Company: **Job Title:**

Section II - Qualitative Elements			
Offer Component	**Importance Ranking**	**Description**	
		Offer #1	Offer #2
Job Content			
Organizational Culture			
Work Environment			
Availability of Feedback			
Growth Potential			
Location			
Commute Time			
Travel Requirements			
Relocation Requirements (Present and Future)			
Number of Hours per Week			
Daily Start / End Times			
Start Date			
Other - Explain			

Section III – Quantitative Elements					
Offer Component	Importance Ranking	Offer #1		Offer #2	
		Company Cost	Your Cost	Company Cost	Your Cost
Salary					
Signing Bonus					
Other Bonuses					
Commission					
Profit Sharing					
Health Benefits					
Medical					
Dental					
Vision					
Other – Explain					
401-K / Retirement Plan					
Paid Time Off (PTO)					
Vacation					
Holidays					
Sick Days					
Other - Explain					
Stipend / Reimbursement					
Relocation					
Education					
Travel					
Expense					
Parking					
Gas					
Performance Reviews					
Other Perks (Cell Phone, Car, Computer, etc)					
Total Costs					

Section IV – Side-by-Side Comparison

Offer #1		Offer #2	
Pro's	Con's	Pro's	Con's

Setting the Stage to Negotiate by Email

First, congratulations. You've received an offer! Now, the more difficult news: the job search process isn't quite over yet. It's time to think over the offer, compare it with your other options, and most importantly: negotiate.

If you've just received a job offer, especially over email, crafting a quick message is a way to strike while the iron is hot for salary negotiation. It's best to keep your salary negotiation emails polite, professional, and direct. You want to demonstrate that you are thoughtful and organized and respect your supervisor's time. He also recommends striking a tone of thankfulness for the opportunity you've been given and avoiding taking a pushy or entitled manner.

As to the specifics – here's how to respond to the offer you've received:

Step 1: Thank the employer for the offer
The hiring manager needs to know that you're genuinely excited and grateful to take this offer. The language most appropriate to use in this email is phrases about working together. You are excited about working together at this company. You are also looking forward to working together to find a salary and benefits package suitable for both of you. You can even restate the offer in their terms, using a sentence like, "I am very grateful for your offer of [salary], but..."

Step 2: State your counter-offer
The number you state in the email is the jumping-off point for negotiations and not necessarily the number you expect will ultimately be offered to you. Utilize a tone that is respectful, polite, and professional. It's also important to remember that most employers expect a counter-offer and have wiggle room built to most first job offers. Test drive a few phrases (below) to see what works best. Here are some effective phrases and some to avoid:

145

Effective Phrases

"Based on my previous compensation package, my ultimate goal is to remain whole..."

"Is there any wiggle room?"

"If it's not too sensitive, do you mind if I ask you what the salary range is for this role?"

"Can we discuss the other components of the compensation plan?"

"How willing are you to..."

Ineffective Phrases

"I will not accept anything less than X."

"I need a higher salary to pay my bills."

Step 3: Back yourself up

The number you ask for doesn't mean much if you can't back it up with research and justification. Research is one of the most important things you can do to make your salary negotiation successful. Always cite your sources, primarily if you're relying on numerical information to back up your ask. Candidates often forget to explain why they want or deserve a higher salary. Researchers have found that negotiators that include a reason why they deserve something are 20% more effective than those who don't. **Remember: The company needs to make an offer for you to evaluate it ---- Not the other way around!**

Use the illustration on the next page to plug in your numbers. This will help you set the stage to optimize your best possible offer based on the position *grade level or salary range.*

Salary Negotiation Strategy

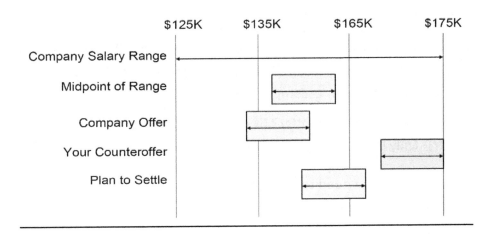

Negotiating Statements When Asked What Your Salary Requirements Are

(Not including search firms)

Your (demands=requirements) responses could be any of or a combination of the following:

• "I think salary is a vital topic, and I would be more than happy to discuss it once a mutual interest has been established." (Get back to discussing your accomplishments)

• "Your company has an excellent reputation, and I'm sure the compensation package will be fair enough to keep me motivated and productive." (By the way, what is the salary range for this position?)

• "Based on my accomplishments and contributions, I would expect to be paid the same level as other executives of my tenure and caliber." (What is the salary range for a person of my caliber?)

• "Regarding compensation, I am flexible and willing to negotiate once we have developed a mutual interest." (Get back to discussing your accomplishments)

• "If we decide that I am the right person for this job, I am sure we will be able to agree on compensation." (Get back to discussing your accomplishments)

• "At this time, I am most interested in determining if I am the right person for this job. If there's a fit, I'm sure salary won't be an issue." (Get back to discussing your accomplishments)

• "Are you making me an offer? (If so, what salary range did you have in mind?)" Only use this response later in the process.

Bottom Line: They need to make an offer for you to evaluate it ---- Not the other way around!

Know your Numbers in advance:
- ✓ What do you really NEED?
- ✓ What do you really WANT?
- ✓ Everything is Negotiable

Second Round Negotiations

Go back to the Hiring Manager (not Human Resources) and say:

• "This is a great opportunity, and I am excited about working with you (or) joining your company."

• "I am inclined to accept your offer; however, there are 3 (or more) items I want to discuss (negotiate) with you."

• "If we can agree on these items, I will be prepared to accept your offer today."

• NOTE: Conduct this negotiation "in person" if possible!

Your Attitude and Assumptions

Your Attitude and Assumptions will determine 80% of the Outcome of Your Salary Negotiations!

Now Set the Stage for Negotiation - Here's Exactly What to Write in your email.

Here is an email template to serve as the primer discussion for your salary negotiation email. This template is ideal because it's brief and to the point, fits the needs of busy hiring managers and recruiters, and is polite, clear, and direct.

Dear [Name of Hiring Manager],

Thank you for offering me the position. I am excited about the opportunity, and I can't wait to start.

I want to discuss the following items on our scheduled call:

1. Guaranteed base salary
2. Bonus/Incentive breakdown
3. Profit-Sharing
4. Sign-on bonus
5. Early performance/salary review
6. Vacation weeks

Remember, this will help prepare the Hiring Manager to be ready to discuss each item you have listed. This is a jumping-off point, and further negotiations may come later. Asking to discuss the offer in brief terms will help you optimize your salary package and get what you are worth.

Conclusion

"Patience is the Path to Your Ambitions"

There's no denying that we live in a world full of instant gratification. As for emailing an employer to follow up on a recent job interview? Anticipate hearing back in several days, if not longer.

With a slight adjustment to your outlook and timeframe, you can still soar through your job search with patience and positivity. Here's how to manage your **R.O.E. = Return On Expectations:**

1. Focus on mini-milestones.
Although the job offer itself ends up being the most important result of your job search, it's helpful to break it down even further to stay the course.

2. Document your job search activities.
Keep track of companies you're applying to, dates and outcomes of phone and office interviews, next steps, and, most importantly, when and with whom you're following up.

3. It's all about numbers.
Landing the "right job" requires several opportunities in your pipeline. Increase your odds by increasing the number of chances with more choices. Stay true to your job search strategy and execute the fundamentals*.

4. Think realistically about timeframes.
You're not the only person eager to land that new job and begin a new chapter in your career. When I worked in corporate recruiting, I had to set expectations with hiring managers who also wanted to make hires in an instant.

5. Understand the Hiring Process.

Would you really want to expedite the process to work for a less-than-stellar employer within three months instead of that amazing employer within five months?

6. Be Patient. Stay Positive.

When it comes to your job search and finding a better opportunity, forget the instant gratification world we live in, and if employers do get back to you rather quickly, remember it's a marathon, not a sprint.

===

Why You Need to Be a Decent Public Speaker

To succeed in today's workplace, you need to become a decent public speaker.

You're at a funeral. Where would you rather be in the room: lying in the casket or standing up front giving the eulogy? Most people pick the casket (at least according to Jerry Seinfeld).

OK, it's a joke, but many people claim they fear public speaking more than death itself.

If this sounds like you, you may not appreciate the following advice: To succeed in the workplace, you need to become a decent public speaker.

Why? Because being able to speak in front of people is a tremendously valuable career skill. Whether you're employed or still hunting, on the first rung of the career ladder, or in the corner office, knowing how to articulate your thoughts to your fellow humans is essential to success.

What better way to shine at job interviews, staff meetings, or business luncheons than to express yourself clearly, confidently, coherently, and concisely? Speaking makes you visible. Speaking makes you memorable. Speaking can even make you look more intelligent. According to a recent study, those who speak up in groups are perceived as more intelligent than those who do not, even when they are less knowledgeable.

Are you terrified of getting up in front of a group and saying something? The only way you're going to get through this is to practice. So consider joining Toastmasters or any other group where you can develop some speaking skills. And consider these 10 Truths of Public Speaking:

1. You will likely not be nervous about speaking in public. Nervousness is normal. Just accept it.
2. Your audience is on your side. Since they're probably terrified of public speaking, too, they respect anyone who does it. They want you to succeed.
3. You don't have to have confidence in yourself to do an excellent job of speaking in public. But you do have to have confidence in your message. This means you need to know your material and what you're talking about.
4. Showing your enthusiasm, belief in what you're saying, and passion for your subject is the best to engage your listeners. Passion perks people up.
5. As counter-intuitive as it may sound, the most effective way to calm your fear is to look directly at your listeners and talk to them individually. Their bright shining faces will give you the courage to go on.
6. Making a mistake (dropping your notes, stumbling over your words, forgetting a point) can endear you to an audience. So please don't make a big deal of it. Smile, apologize, correct yourself, and carry on.
7. Don't memorize your speech. It will feed your fear that you'll forget something. It will pressure you to be "perfect," which is both impossible and a recipe for anxiety. Be your genuine, courteous, engaged, humble-but-knowledgeable self.
8. Know your audience. What does your audience want to hear? What are their priorities? Focusing on their concerns instead of

yours is another good way to lift yourself out of your pit of anxiety.

9. The most effective messages are the simple ones. So, don't bury your audience under a mountain of data. Two or three key points are about all most groups can easily digest in one sitting. They will thank you for this.

10. Know your purpose. Why are you speaking? Usually, it's to inform, educate, or entertain. However, you may have a hidden (even to yourself) agenda: to impress people. This is natural, but if you are speaking only to impress, it will show, and your listeners will be turned off. Impressing an audience results from doing an excellent job of informing, educating, or entertaining (Refer to #1 through #9). That's the key to effective speaking to anyone.

What is Executive Career Transition Coaching?

I have been asked by many clients and friends, "What is executive career transition coaching?" A simple and straight answer would be the International Coaching Federation (ICF) definition: Coaching is partnering with clients in a thought-provoking and creative process that inspires them to maximize their personal and professional potential.

This definition is elegantly simple, but it is packed with many complexities. Two of those complexities, especially when coaching high-level executives, are related to the driver/objective and the length of the engagement.

Let's talk about the driver/objective of the engagement first. When people initiate a coaching engagement, it usually falls into four categories. The one I am most familiar with is coaching executives in career transition or those individuals that are leaving a company in the near future. ***This level of coaching is defined in Four Phases.***

Four Phases of Executive Career Transition Coaching

1. Assessing your leadership skills, evaluating the current market conditions and landscape, and creating a customized and strategic Job Search Marketing Plan™.
2. Executing the plan (strategy) through active Marketplace Communication (networking) critical talent, top leadership, CEO succession planning.
3. Securing first job interviews and comprehensive Mock Interview Training and Salary Negotiation concepts and strategies to close the deal on your optimal salary package.
4. Closing out your job search and New Job Assimilation/On-Boarding Success for the first 100 days.

The Bottom Line

Executive Career Transition Coaching is a limited-time engagement lasting 6-12 months. A professional career coach will assist, teach and guide you through the process of conducting a professional job search campaign. Here is a list of deliverables you should expect from a reputable career coach:

- Management competency and skills assessment
- Resumé and cover letter development
- Creation of job search marketing strategy and guidance on how to uncover the hidden jobs
- Perfecting your messaging, branding, and highest and best use
- Alternative career options, such as self-employment, consulting, business, and franchise ownership (Plan B is the new Plan A)
- Secrets to mastering professional networking
- Introductions to professional connections
- Utilizing executive search firms and staying on a recruiter's radar
- Mock Interview Training (in person or via Zoom)
- Optimal salary negotiation to get paid what you are worth
- New job assimilation and "on-boarding"

Professional career coaches will provide unbiased opinions and advice regarding the next steps and how to accomplish them. They assist and guide in teaching the skills for negotiation of a better compensation package.

Some career coaches will provide professional introductions to help their clients expand their network and connectivity to key executives and professionals. They should provide the necessary emotional support to get their clients through the job transition.

Above all, a career coach will hold their clients accountable and keep them focused on achieving critical weekly activity goals.

Hiring a good coach will typically speed up the job search process and can save you weeks and months of time-wasting mistakes.

In Summary

The ultimate path to mastering your career is to understand that it's a wise move to utilize an effective learning and career coaching system to ensure and accelerate your success. Simply put, there are two major components to people's decision-making process—emotional and logical.

There is no question that a person in transition is surrounded by all kinds of emotionally driven thoughts. Given a little time, the emotional side will subside and be taken over by logic. That is the time to make the hard decisions. The sooner you get there, the sooner you will get employed.

Keep in mind that the most significant career growth and learning in life takes place in the context of supportive, trusted advisor relationships.

No matter what your circumstances may be, working in partnership with a career coach will have a profound impact and value. If you would like some assistance, we're available to help you.

HIRE Consulting Services (HCS) Career Coaching for Executives and Professionals in Career Transition

Do you need help with the fundamentals of conducting a professional job search campaign and managing your career path?

Schedule a 30-minute consultation with HCS. Send an email with your resumé and cover letter to: info@HireConsulting.com. Please include your two best days and times that you're available to talk by phone? We will get back to you with a good time to schedule the appointment.

==

HCS Published Book Online Resource Documents

The Interview Mindset (2022) and **Keys to C SUITE** (2018) reference several documents that are available to download for your job search on the **Hire Consulting Services** (HCS) website link below:
https://hireconsulting.com/career-transition-resource-documents/

==

Companies and Organizations that are interested in learning more about HCS Strategic Recruiting Solutions, Talent Selection and Optimization with The Predictive Index Behavior Assessment, please contact HCS directly:

HIRE Consulting Services:
► **760-230-4301 (San Diego Office)**
► **Info@HireConsulting.com**
► **https://hireconsulting.com/contact/**

mindset

[miynd-set]   *noun*

The driving force in the quest for success and achievement. A mindset that combines discipline, strength, confidence, and ambition is a powerful mindset. This can achieve anything it sets its sights on.

Bonus Chapter

Top 10 Leadership Mindsets

A leadership mindset involves having certain attitudes, beliefs, and expectations that create the foundation of who you are, how you lead others, and how you interact with and influence your colleagues. This mindset is essential to hone because it is the driving component of everything you do within your job.

Four elemental leadership mindsets—**growth, inclusive, agile, and enterprise**—are critical to being a successful leader today. A growth mindset is foundational to leadership success because it supports the premise that people can learn, grow, and expand their skills. Here are the Top 10 Leadership Mindsets:

1. **Honesty, Ethics, and Integrity**
   These three characteristics are unquestionably a supreme quality of leadership.

2. **Confidence**
   As a leader, you have to exude confidence.

3. **Inspire Others**
   Lead by example by inspiring your followers.

4. **Commitment and Passion**
   Be passionate and roll up your sleeves to demonstrate commitment.

5. **Great Communicator**
   You must be able to communicate your message effectively.

6. **Decision-Making Capabilities**
   Decisions made by leaders have a profound impact on their people and teams.

7. **Accountability**

   Everyone on the team is accountable for what they are doing, starting with the leader.

8. **Delegation and Empowerment**

   Empower your followers and delegate tasks to them with trust.

9. **Creativity and Innovation**

   Innovation distinguishes between a leader and a follower.

10. **Empathy**

    Leaders should develop empathy with their followers.

About Mark James, CPC

Mark James, CPC, is the founder and president of **HIRE Consulting Services**, (HCS) established in 1999. Mark is a Certified Personnel Consultant and the author of the best-selling book **"Keys to the C Suite: Unlock the Doors to Executive Career Path Success."** He is equipped with over 25 years of experience in Executive Career Management Coaching, Outplacement, and Executive Search Consulting. He has been a Certified Partner with **The Predictive Index** since 2016.

Mark excels in executive search consulting and coaching business professionals and executives who are currently in career transition or planning to make a career change.

As an Executive Career Transition Coach, Mark works with clients to define their skills and competencies and develop a strategy to conduct a professional job search campaign. "Our common goal at HCS is to find the right company that values the talents of my clients." Every meeting, discussion, and phone call is made with the singular purpose of helping you discover the keys and utilize the tools to help you secure a more fulfilled and productive career path.

As an Executive Search Recruiter, Mark partners with successful and growing companies that need a competitive recruiting edge to enable them to find, assess, and hire great talent. HCS Strategic Recruiting Solutions search process helps client companies locate, assess, and recruit exceptional leaders in a variety of industries, functions, and disciplines. Mark accomplishes this by increasing interview and hiring accuracy while adhering to the Highest Recruiting Industry Ethical Standards.

Made in the USA
Middletown, DE
03 July 2022

68206468R00099